WRITERS ON WRITING

Top Christian Writers Share Their Secrets
for Getting Published

Edited by James N. Watkins

wesleyan
publishing
house

Indianapolis, Indiana

© 2005 by Wesleyan Publishing House
Published by Wesleyan Publishing House
Indianapolis, Indiana 46250
Printed in the United States of America

ISBN-13: 978-0-89827-312-0
ISBN-10: 0-89827-312-9

Edited by James N. Watkins.

Library of Congress Cataloging-in-Publication Data

Writers on writing : top Christian writers share their secrets for getting published / James N. Watkins, editor.
    p. cm.
  Includes bibliographical references.
  ISBN-13: 978-0-89827-312-0 (pbk.)
  1. Christian literature--Authorship. 2. Christian literature--Publishing. I. Watkins, James N.
  BR44.W75 2006
  808'.06623--dc22
                    2005024617

CONTENTS

PREFACE

Words are sacred. They deserve respect. If you get the right ones, in the right order, you can nudge the world a little.

—Tom Stoppard

"In the beginning was the Word, and the Word was with God, and the Word was God" (John 1:1).

Words, especially *written* words, have always been powerfully used by God.

Moses received God's written words in the form of the Ten Commandments, which have endured as a cornerstone of civil law and personal morality for three and a half thousand years.

Prophets were commanded to pen eternal warnings, judgments, and truths. These written decrees, discovered by Josiah, led to the reformation of Israel.

God himself wrote on the palace wall that Nebuchadnezzar's kingdom had been "weighed on the scales and found wanting" (Dan. 5:27).

The New Testament begins with a long list of written names, proving that Jesus Christ was of the lineage of David. He was born in Bethlehem, just as the prophets had penned, because of the need for a written census. Jesus studied in the Temple school from the hand-copied Pentateuch. Throughout his life, Christ confronted friends and foes with the written words of his Father. He wrote a mysterious message in the sand that stopped those determined to stone a woman caught in adultery.

Early Christians were eager to take eternal truth and frame it into words that could be understood and would endure throughout time.

Luke wrote, "Many have undertaken to draw up an account of the things that have been fulfilled among us, just as they were handed down to us by those who from the first were eyewitnesses and servants of the word. Therefore, since I myself have carefully investigated everything from the beginning, it seemed good also to me to write an orderly account for you, most excellent Theophilus, so that you may know the certainty of the things you have been taught" (Luke 1:1–4).

And 1 John 5:13 says, "I write these things to you who believe in the name of the Son of God so that you may know that you have eternal life."

The Reformation was influenced by Martin Luther's tracts. The great revivals of England and North America were inspired by John Wesley's books. And the effects of the written words of Augustine, Thomas à Kempis, Charles Spurgeon, A. W. Tozer, C. S. Lewis, William Barclay, and thousands more continue today.

God has always used the written word to communicate his truth.

There are those who argue that the written word will soon be replaced by electronic media. But even the majority of new technology, such as digital audio and video, the Internet, instant messaging, etc., are firmly based in the written word, albeit pixels rather than pages.

I'm convinced that the written word will always be the most effective form of mass communication because it is the most personal. It is a one-on-one experience between you and the author. I was honored to win a *Campus Life* Book of the Year award but was immediately humbled by one of the teen judges who wrote, "Jim is not an author." Ouch! But then she went on to write, "No, it's like he's sharing with you over Diet Cokes at McDonalds." Writing is an intimate conversation between you and the reader.

Reading is personal as well because you choose the time and place. You read at your own speed. You can back up and reread a section that you particularly enjoy—or can't understand. You can dog-ear pages, underline, highlight, or copy and paste helpful sections. God has used the impact and intimacy of the written word for nearly four thousand years, and continues to use pages and pixels to communicate his truth. Today, in fact, religious writing is the fastest growing segment of publishing.

"The Word" needs new authors who will pen his timeless Word in contemporary forms that will effectively communicate to today's world.

We've assembled some of the most effective writers, editors, and writing instructors today to help you continue that lineage of the written word with this book. My books and yours may not be on the best-seller list for thousands of years like Moses' and Paul's, but our writing can make an eternal difference in the lives of those who read our words.

JAMES N. WATKINS

THE WRITER

1

INSPIRATION FOR CHRISTIAN WRITING

Bonnie Perry

I write only when I'm inspired. Fortunately I'm inspired at 9 o'clock every morning.

–William Faulkner

W hy write? The question begs an answer, even from those of us who have chosen to make a career of getting words on paper in some form or fashion. After all, it's not that much fun, this writing stuff. I have a postcard bearing a quote from Gene Fowler pinned above my desk. "Writing is easy;" it says. "All you do is sit staring at a blank sheet of paper until drops of blood form on your forehead."

The easy answer to my question would be something noble sounding, such as "I believe in the power of words." How true. In fact, one of my favorite authors, Emily Dickinson, wrote, "A word is dead when it is said, some say. I say it just begins to live that day." It's a profound thought.

Profound, but not enough. For believers, God must figure into the equation. I think God believes in the power of words. The psalmist wrote, "My heart is stirred by a noble theme as I recite my verses for the king; my tongue is the pen of a skillful writer" (Ps. 45:1). Better, but still not an answer that completely satisfies me.

So, as a Christian, I come back to the question, why write? I got my answer one gorgeous spring afternoon in Kansas City—when I wanted to be outside enjoying the weather but instead sat inside at my desk, glumly preparing a workshop for a writers' conference. That day, God gave me my answer as I was randomly flipping through my Bible, halfheartedly looking for inspiration. I call my epiphany, "Moses and the Three Writers."

> Now Moses was tending the flock of Jethro . . . and he led the flock to the far side of the desert . . . to the mountain of God. There the angel of the LORD appeared to him in flames of fire from within a bush. . . .
>
> God called to him from within the bush, "Moses! Moses!"
>
> And Moses said, "Here I am."
>
> "Do not come any closer," God said. Take off your sandals, for the place where you are standing is holy ground. . . ."
>
> At this, Moses hid his face, because he was afraid to look at God.
>
> The LORD said, "I have indeed seen the misery of my people in Egypt. I have heard them crying out because of their slave drivers, and I am concerned about their suffering. So I have come down to rescue them from the hand of the Egyptians and to bring them up out of that land into a good and spacious land, a land flowing with milk and honey . . ." (Exod. 3:1–8).

For many believers, this story of Moses is a familiar narrative. We've heard sermon after sermon on this passage of Scripture. That spring day as I read the account (wondering why God led me there), the words said something unexpected to me. I believe it has something unexpected to say to writers as well.

Moses was tending the flock of Jethro . . . and he led the flock to the far side of the desert . . . to the mountain of God. Moses in the desert. In the spiritual vernacular, desert equals tough times. Moses was in the *rear* of the desert, so far back he may have believed there was no way out. He had sojourned in that desert forty years or so, and was accustomed to the place. It was comfortable for him. Maybe he wasn't even looking for a way out. Life wasn't so bad there. He spent his days herding sheep. Week after week. Month after month. Alone in the quiet. It was quiet there in the desert, at the foot of the mountain. It was so quiet Moses could hear the faintest whisper of the wind or the slightest stirring of the breeze. It was so quiet he could hear the very voice of God.

I knew a writer once. (Let's call her Writer One.) She was a young mom, tired but mostly happy. Writer One decided to crawl out of bed a little early, before her three kids woke up, to sit alone in her living room. It was quiet there in the living room. It was so quiet Writer One could hear the smallest creaking of the floor or the gentle breathing of the children. It was so quiet she could hear the very voice of God.

I knew another writer once. (Let's call him Writer Two). He'd been a writer for a long time. Writer Two found some trails close to his home, where he could walk in the woods. It was quiet there among the trees. It was so quiet Writer Two could hear all the forest sounds. It was so quiet he could hear the very voice of God.

I knew a third writer once. (Let's call her Writer Three.) Her kids were grown, and her secret dream was to write stories. Writer Three worked from her home office. It was quiet there at her desk. It was so quiet Writer Three could hear the humming of the computer and the ticking of the desk clock. It was so quiet she could hear the very voice of God.

Let's think again about Moses at the foot of God's mountain. In the quiet, God said, *Moses, Moses . . . take off your shoes . . . you are on holy ground . . . because I'm here.*

God transforms the most unlikely places into holy ground.

Writer One heard the murmur of God in her heart. "I'm here in your living room," He said. "This is holy ground." She lay face down on her carpet, with toys and cookie crumbs all around, and soaked in the presence of God.

Writer Two walked a long time through the woods that day. He listened to the birds, the wind, and the water cry out the goodness of God. It became a holy place.

Writer Three sat at her desk completely still in front of the laptop. She didn't fill the silence with words of supplication, intercession, or even praise and thanksgiving. She simply enjoyed his presence, and let him fill her in a way she hadn't experienced for years.

In the biblical story, while Moses stood on holy ground, silent in the presence of Almighty God, something unprecedented happened to him. God spoke. *I have indeed seen the misery of my people . . . I see their slave drivers . . . I am aware of their suffering . . . So I have come to deliver them to a good and a spacious land.*

God's message resonates through the ages. Writers One, Two, and Three, heard it. "I have seen the misery of my people . . . I am aware of their suffering . . . I see their slave drivers . . . rejection, loneliness, insecurity, fear. So I have come to deliver them to a good and a spacious land—and you are my mouthpiece."

For Moses, God proceeded to lay out the mission. He went over it detail by detail in Moses' quiet place, where he could hear the voice of God. For the writers, God did the same:

To Writer One, with her face buried in the carpet, God was very direct. "Come back tomorrow. I want to spend time with you."

To Writer Two, walking in the woods, God didn't say anything specific. But the writer felt refreshed and went home to finish the last chapter of the novel he shelved months ago.

To Writer Three, God said something seemingly unrelated, "Go make things right with your son, who is a prodigal. Ask him to forgive you for your anger."

The writers had their marching orders. So did Moses. Consider the rest of the story:

> Moses answered, "What if they do not believe me or listen to me and say, 'The LORD did not appear to you'?"
>
> Then the LORD said to him, "What is that in your hand?"
>
> "A staff," he replied.
>
> The LORD said, "Throw it on the ground."
>
> Moses threw it on the ground and it became a snake, and he ran from it. Then the LORD said to him, "Reach out your hand and take it by the tail . . . that they may believe that the LORD, the God of their fathers . . . has appeared to you" (Exod. 4:1–5).

After hearing God's instructions, Moses replied, "What if they do not believe me or listen to me?"

Can you resonate with Moses' objections? I can. As writers, we fight it all the time. What if I'm not good enough, God? It's a fear that haunts us every time we stare at the blank page.

God's response to Moses is provocative; it comes in the form of a question. *What is that in your hand?*

A staff.

Throw it down. It became a serpent, alive with the power of God. And Moses ran away.

I believe God is challenging writers in a similar manner, "By the way, what's that in your hand? That pen (or keyboard, as it were)? Don't hold on too tightly. Lay it down at the foot of the cross and watch it come alive with the power of God!"

The Lord didn't leave it at that, with Moses throwing down the tool he used every day and then running the other way. "Stretch out your hand and grasp it by the tail," He said. Pick it up, Moses. By the tail (because the power is in the head.) Pick it up and use it for the Kingdom.

Writer One got up from the living room floor. She wrote articles in her spare time; many of them appeared in the local newspaper and some in small magazines.

Writer Two returned from the woods, pulled the long-forgotten novel from his desk drawer and finished it. His book was a bestseller.

Writer Three spent her evenings writing stories. Though they were never published, her son kept them, and the legacy impacted her family for many years.

The Lord challenged Moses. He challenged the three writers. He challenges me. I believe He is calling us to throw down our gifts at the foot of the cross, watch them come alive with the power of God, pick them up, and use them for the Kingdom.

Why write? For one reason alone. He told Moses. He tells us. "That they may believe in the LORD, the God of their fathers, Abraham, Isaac and Jacob."

In our quiet place, so quiet that we can hear the very voice of God, especially the voice of God, He whispers to us with His own question. "Will you obey?"

WHEN INSPIRATION WON'T COME

Ron McClung

What does a writer do when inspiration won't come? What happens when you run out of ideas? How do you pull out of a writing slump when nothing seems to work?

STIMULATING IDEAS

FILING SYSTEM

I have used a number of techniques across the years to help me with this problem. Developing a good filing system is a big asset. Years ago, I started filing quotations, articles, and excerpts from my reading, alphabetically by topic. Consequently, I have file folders on hundreds of subjects from A to Z. If my well of inspiration runs dry and if I can at least decide on a subject, I can open a file and see what some other people have said. Often this provokes thoughts around which to develop an article.

CURRENT EVENTS

Being aware of what is happening around you is another way to stimulate ideas. If people are already thinking about some event that is current in the news, and if you can find a way to relate it to the truth of God's Word, you can discover a beginning point for an article. We also have many holidays and special observations in our culture that lend themselves to biblically oriented observations.

THE INTERNET

It is possible to research almost anything on the Internet. So if an idea comes to mind, about which you don't know enough to write, yet your curiosity is stimulated, you can track down information on the Internet. Speaking of which, there are Web sites with lists of events that happened in history on every day of the year. You might be surprised how many things have occurred in history on this very calendar date. Some of them may well have to do with the Church or some moral issue.

Even if they are totally secular in nature, you may find the seed for an inspirational article. For instance, if it happens to be the day when Thomas Edison received the patent on one of his inventions, a writer can begin with that fact and go on to talk about the importance of perseverance, a trait that Edison seemed to have in abundance. If the date in question happens to be one on which a famous person was born or died, and that person is known for some quality worth emulating, or some characteristics to avoid, you may have an article in the making.

PERSONAL EXPERIENCE

Put something of yourself in an article. Stop and think about what is going on in your life. You may feel totally uninspired, but just think about what has happened to you in the past week. Whom have you seen? Where have you gone? What have you done?

I took my own advice recently and meditated for awhile on what had been happening in my life. At first I thought it had been a fairly dull week, with nothing that inspired me to write. Then I remembered something I saw on television, a unique idea about helping men relate better to their wives or sweethearts. With just a few clicks on the computer mouse, I had more information about the topic. It was enough to inspire me to begin writing, relate it to some biblical ideas, and before long another article was done.

With a good filing system, along with keen powers of observation, and a curiosity that pursues an idea, you need not be without inspiration for long.

2

THE IMPACT OF CHRISTIAN WRITING

James L. Garlow

Write this down for the next generation so people
not yet born will praise God.

—Psalm 102:18, The Message

Your words matter.

The great temptation as a Christian writer is to believe that your words are meaningless. "Nobody reads what I write," you may have thought. "My work won't amount to much."

You couldn't be more wrong. Words matter, all of them. And the words we write to advance the Kingdom matter most of all.

In the fourth century, a single word mattered enough that it caused the bishop of Alexandria to be deposed and exiled. That one word was so important that it caused the emperor Constantine to convene a council of the church to consider its meaning. The bishop was Athanasius. The word was *incarnation*. And the document produced by that council, the Nicene Creed, is now read every Sunday in churches all over the world.

Words matter. Your words matter.

On October 31, 1517, a Roman Catholic priest posted 2,717 words on the door of a church in Wittenberg, Germany. They were mere words, only 2,717 of them, but they mattered a great deal. The priest was Martin Luther. The document was the Ninety-Five Theses, and it ignited a reformation that shook the foundations of Western society.

His words had power. Your words have power.

Two centuries later, an Anglican minister toyed with the meaning behind two simple words: *perfect love*. Those words caused him to be ridiculed, criticized, barred from every pulpit in England, and even stoned. The minister's name was John Wesley, and he led a revival movement called Methodism that swept through England and spread to America. Millions of lives have been changed by the power of those words and the man who had the courage to continue preaching and writing them in spite of fierce opposition.

His words influenced many, and so will yours.

People fight to control words, often ruthlessly, simply because words have the power to influence. Even now, the words *terror, choice,* or *family* influence emotions, stir reactions. It's true, isn't it, that God did not send his Justice or his Authority or his Knowledge or even his Peace to save the world. It was the Word that became flesh and dwelt among us. It was the Word that revealed God to us. It is our words that reveal Him now.

Given the power of words, described in Proverbs as either the cause of death or the source of life, it seems strange that we devalue them as we do.

George Orwell truly saw the future in his novel *1984*. He predicted that the world would be held in slavery not by the force of arms but by the corruption of words. "Freedom is slavery" was the motto of his imagined state. We are living there now. We have corrupted the meaning of words, and we suffer the result.

Corporations do not fire their employees anymore. They *restructure* themselves. The Congressman did not lie, rather he *misspoke*. Adultery is now *fallen out of love*, homosexual relationships now *alternate lifestyles*. Misleading translations, as these, echo Goebbels' inscription above the entrance to Auschwitz: "Work Makes Free." Word-tricks numb a culture, creating a false sense of unity and peace.

Words that do not lend themselves readily to translation are edited out of usage altogether. *Sin, grace, repentance, judgment*. One wonders if these concepts are appropriate for our present time, a time that perverts the true meaning of words. Yet in this world where nothing seems to matter, we stand against the culture with—words. In a world of lost meaning, we offer hope, forgiveness, purpose—just words.

Words that matter.

In the middle of the nineteenth century, a series of short stories were published in the abolitionist paper *The National Era* illustrating the harsh realities of slavery. The author of the series was a tiny, middle-aged Harriet Beecher Stowe, the wife of a theology professor and mother of six children, after having a son die of cholera a few years prior. She and her husband, Calvin E. Stowe, would only see three of their children outlive them. Harriet began writing these stories of *Life Among the Lowly* because she was outraged by the passing of the Fugitive Slave Act of 1850, an act that criminalized the safe-harboring of runway slaves.

Although Harriet never lived in the South, being born in Connecticut, she moved to Cincinnati with her family when she was twenty one years old just across the Ohio River from the slave state of Kentucky. Cincinnati is where she met Calvin, a professor at Lane Theological Seminary where her Father was president, and where we trace her connection with the Underground Railroad and slaves' rights. In Cincinnati Harriet learned that the family servant, Zillah, was a runaway slave. Calvin and Harriet's brother Henry Ward Beecher helped Zillah locate the nearest station of the covert railway. It was also there on the banks of the Ohio where Harriet obtained most of her material for the short newspaper sketches, stories of physical and sexual abuse, images of slave mothers running across the frozen river with their children to escape the slave trade.

In 1850, Calvin took a position at Bowdoin College and the family moved to Brunswick, Maine. On June 2, 1851, the first sketch of *Uncle Tom's Cabin* appeared in *The National Era* and with each installment the anticipation from readers grew. Stowe wrote forty episodes altogether before the Boston publisher, John P. Jewett, picked them up and published them as a two volume book in 1852. Six thousand copies sold overnight with three presses running around the clock. Three Hundred thousand copies sold in the first year. For the first time slaves were portrayed as fellow humans, making the evils of slavery much more atrocious. The Nation stood divided on this issue—some lauding Stowe, some cursing her—and would go to war with itself a few years later. Legend tells that when Harriet finally met President Lincoln in 1862, midway through the Civil War, he remarked to her "So you're the little woman who wrote the book that started this great war!"

Uncle Tom's Cabin was a success beyond the United States and earned Stowe international acclaim. It stands today as a novel that greatly influenced the course of America and as a haunting reminder of our dim past. Harriet Beecher Stowe, a tiny, New England woman, pushed an entire country to decide where it stood on the issue of slavery with mere words.

Her words had influence. Your words have influence.

A few years after Mrs. Stowe published her powerful work, a boy was born in a pastor's family in Wellsville, New York. That boy would move on with his family to Missouri, Michigan, the Dakota Territory, finally settling in Kansas where he composed a work that has reached millions of people around the world. The boy was Charles Monroe Sheldon and most people at the present time that have been touched by his work have no idea who he was.

Charles Sheldon received his theological training from Brown University and Andover Theological Seminary, and following in the foot steps of his father, he entered the pastorate. His first church was a small Congregationalist community in Waterbury, Vermont. After two years of fruitful ministry there, he traveled west to Topeka, Kansas, and became the pastor of the Central Congregationalist Church. Just before the turn of the century, Reverend Sheldon instituted in a new way of preaching to stir students' interest in the Sunday night service. Instead of orating the typical sermon, Sheldon weaved the main theological points that he wanted to convey with the story of a young pastor, Rev. Henry Maxwell, and his wife. Written in novel form, Rev. Sheldon read his story serially ending each Sunday night in a moment of suspense, which hooked his audience and reassured their return the following week.

The response to this sermon series was phenomenal. Students traveled from around Kansas to hear him. A religious magazine based out of Chicago, *Advance*, published the series in weekly installments. The reaction from readers was so great that it eventually came into to print in book form entitled *In His Steps*. Several other publishers picked up the series and printed books of their own. It is estimated that since it came out in 1896, world-wide sales have reached close to thirty million copies. Here's the amazing part, neither Charles Sheldon nor his family ever received a penny of royalties for his work. He never copyrighted the material. His motivation was not wealth or admiration. He wrote *In His Steps* to call believers to truly follow the example of Jesus.

In the beginning chapter of Sheldon's novel, Rev. Henry Maxwell meets a vagabond character, a *tramp*, whose final monologue and death helps to refocus this young pastor on the true calling of God. As the vagabond stands before the shocked congregation, he poses the simple question, "What would Jesus do?" Now you all know who Charles Monroe Sheldon is, don't you. You may not have though if it weren't for a youth minister who created woven bracelets for teenagers, embroidered with the acronym WWJD. The immense popularity of the WWJD bracelet brought the spotlight back to Sheldon's classic story. His great-grandson Garret Sheldon has written an updated version of the novel along with a screenplay. Copyrights have no doubt been obtained for these new works.

Charles Monroe Sheldon's humble words thrive today, encouraging students across the world to walk as Jesus did. Your words have the same potential to grip the hearts of so many and change lives.

Your words matter.

Christian material is the fastest growing market in the publishing world. The Word is getting out there. Your words are getting out there and have the power to influence the nations for Christ. When you get discouraged in your writing, remember these stories of humble writers and explosive results. Keep writing. Keep serving.

PAUL AND APOLLOS

 James L. Garlow

Two figures of the formative period of the Christian church provide us with an interesting contrast: the written word versus the oral speech. Acts 18 introduces us to a Jew named Apollos, an educated man well-versed in the Scripture. He came from Alexandria preaching of Jesus and the baptism of John the Baptist. In Ephesus, Aquila and Priscilla taught him the complete story of Jesus as the Messiah, and he became very strong in public debates against the Jews, using Scripture to prove that Jesus was the promised King. His persuasive speech made Apollos very popular in his day as he watered the scattered seed that Paul had sown.

Paul, on the contrary, was not bold in speech, but his writing possessed the voice of a lion. Along with his many missionary travels, imprisonments, and beatings, he wrote thirteen books of the twenty seven collected for the New Testament. Although audiences were often disappointed with Paul's oral teaching style—self-admitted—his writings were powerful and still fill the earth with Christ's glory.

But what sets apart Paul from Apollos?

Apollos was a skilled orator, much more skilled than Paul, but Paul's influence touches us today because he wrote it down. He wrote down the words of God and they live to this day. We don't know any of Apollos' arguments for Jesus as the Christ because they don't exist presently in writing. His words have passed away with time, but Paul's written words live on, influencing nations of every language.

Don't be an Apollos. Write!

3

THE SELF-IDENTITY OF A CHRISTIAN WRITER

Norman G. Wilson

I want to go on living even after my death! And therefore I am grateful to God for giving me this gift, this possibility of developing myself and of writing, of expressing all that is in me.

—Anne Frank

Joseph Telushkin tells the story of a Hasidic rabbi named Zusha, who used to say, "When I die and come before the heavenly court, if they ask me 'Zusha, why were you not as great as Abraham?' I will not be afraid. I will say that I was not born with Abraham's intellectual capabilities. And if they ask me, 'Why were you not like Moses?' I will say that I did not have his leadership skills. But when they ask me, 'Zusha, why were you not Zusha?' for that I will have no answer."

That, perhaps, is the most pressing question a Christian writer must face. Why were you not you? Not why were you not Charles Coleson or Chuck Swindoll or Philip Yancey. But, why were you not yourself? Your ability to answer that question will be determined by how well you know yourself.

Most of us tend to hide our self behind thin smiles and gold-sealed certificates, a fragile structure protected by thick layers of deception. The search for identity—scaling the ranges and ridges of personality and accomplishment—is the epic quest each of us take in the hunt for the answer to the pervasive question, who am I? It could be a long and rigorous journey. One that is seldom completed alone.

Among our constant companions are questions. Questions which help to peel back the outer layers by which we cloak our true self. As a human being, we might ask, what is my worth? As a son or daughter, what am I to become? As a father, what should I do? As a Christian writer, who am I? The answer will be found not in our accomplishments or rewards, but within our ability to recognize the purpose of God for which we were born.

IDENTITY LOST

The journey begins in the obvious places of work and family, but identity is not found hiding in the open, in what we do each day, our work. Your identity as a Christian writer is not found in your occupation. Whether you program software, file papers, or pour concrete, your identity remains separate. The English language, as it often does, has muddied the meaning of the word vocation. In its root form vocation is not synonymous with occupation. Vocation derives from the Latin word *vocare*, translated as calling. Occupation, as defined, is what we do day to day that occupies our time. Your occupation may not always be in line with your true calling. The key is to find an occupation that leans in the same direction as your vocation, for many times our calling is not provisionally lucrative and there are empty stomachs at home.

David was a king. Luke, a skilled physician. Isaiah, a prophet. All followed a deep calling on their lives and wrote down what they felt, what they saw, what they knew was to come. Writing may be a sincere calling you have felt lying dormant in the recesses of your dreams, but you have never pursued it because it was not your occupation. What has been said about speaking—some people speak because they have something to say—others because they have to say something—could also be said about writers. A true writer does not write because it is an occupation, but because it is an internal compulsion.

As a writer, though, you must be wary of finding your identity in your writing. "I am loved because of what I write. I am accepted because of my ability." We must detach our identity from the intensely personal work of writing, especially the success and acceptance of our work. When we find our identity in our writing, our self-esteem rises and falls with each publication. The question of motive will shine light on this problem. Are you writing as an outpouring of your calling, or are you writing to be known, to be recognized and famous. The false self, a mirage of expectation and doubt, constantly searches for its own glory, a point well explained by psychologist Karen Horney. The false self desires to be loved and worshiped forever. Your writing will always be stifled as long as you use it to grasp at immortality.

While the false self feasts on praise, your identity as a Christian writer is not found in the opinions of others. It is easy to live and die by the pens of cruel critics or exacting editors. But the murmurs behind your back are not the sum of your worth, not even if they are words of admiration. Clergy feel similar pressure as writers, the need to be wise, to be eloquent. The weight of which can be unbearable. Writers and pastors deal with the promotion of ideas, the dispersal of knowledge. As we do this we stretch our arms outward in vulnerability, silently awaiting the arrows of criticism. We must not let public opinion polls deride our writing, nor the clergy his preaching. Criticism should inform us but never defeat us.

IDENTITY FOUND

True self-identity, as a Christian writer, just as with all human beings, is found in relationship with the living, loving Almighty God. The identity you have been searching tirelessly for is you, stripped of acclamation and esteem, criticism and scorn, loved by God. This isn't just a pat on the head to make you feel like a good little writer. This is the existential reality of what it means to be a child of God, a friend of the Eternal. He pierces false motives, paralyzing fears, and loves you completely, unlike any love you have ever experienced. His love plants seeds of potential deep within your soul. This is your identity as a Christian writer. You are no longer driven to be recognized because you are known, fully, by the Creator of the Universe.

As your identity develops in the process of pursuing your calling, you come to peace with who you are. Rejection slips may still sting but the pain is moderated. Your self worth is no longer attached directly to the number of books published or net profit sales. This new peace makes your writing better. It is not a game of proving your worth but of sharing your heart. The superficial success of your writing is less important than your love for the craft. You may never be on the *New York Times'* best sellers list, but your acclaim comes from fulfilling your calling.

Just because our identity as writers is found in the same loving God, our individual uniqueness is not diminished. God enlivens our personalities and deepens our creativity. The author of personality, the design behind creative arts, does not mold everyone into the same pattern. His love is personal, unique to each of His friends. He loves your wit and her logic. He knows how you love to organize even your junk drawer, and He holds the hand of the carefree. We can get confused, though, when we find our identity in our uniqueness. We are dynamic; we change. Our uniqueness ebbs with each season. When we define our identity from one area of uniqueness in our lives we stunt the development of our true self. The Apostle Paul said that when I was a child I spoke, thought and understood; and it could be added, wrote like a child, and when I became an adult I put away childishness. But even in my maturity my identity has not changed. I am still known and loved of God.

CHARACTERISTICS OF A CHRISTIAN WRITER

While true identity is found in God, the self-identity of a Christian writer is not without a few specific characteristics, subtle features that line the pages of our work. In each trait we find shared qualities and our own unique interpretations.

A COMPANION OF TRUTH

The biggest ally of the Christian writer in this journey is Truth. We do not possess the truth, bottled and stuffed into our knapsacks like some personal possession. We walk alongside of Truth, or better yet, follow its footprints, letting it direct our way. Our friendship with Truth must always be in proper context as well. We are not the defenders of Truth. She needs no defense, not even the strongest of arguments can defeat her. Rather, Truth is our guardian, as she guides our writing away from the swamps of false opinion and malice-laced motives. It is not a matter of rightness or wrongness in a harsh judicial sense with Truth. Truth is graceful.

The reader can sense when you, the writer, are not dealing honestly with a topic or portion of Scripture. When you walk with Truth as a friend, your writing possesses her grace and gentle voice. When you use Truth as a club, shaking the finger of her authority, your writing stiffens and injures the reader.

A COURIER OF HOPE

One tendency of Christian writers is to focus exclusively on "the silver lining" when there is more to life's story than that. Truth asks us to deal with the greater breadth of life's story, while scattering promises of hope across its pages and paragraphs. Hope works its way beneath the surface of our human experiences. To focus solely on the happily-ever-after ending of the story appears Pollyannaish to the reader and weakens the power of the experience. Readers want to understand the crisis of the situation with the knowledge that hope lives. As a Christian writer we must make room for both to happen.

We do have hope. We have not yet arrived at the end of the story, but we do know how the story ends. As we spread this message of hope, may we do it in a way that validates the genuine experiences of our readers.

A MINDFUL MEDIATOR

One of the main jobs of a Christian writer is to translate the abstract concepts of God into concrete metaphors that readers can understand. This work is not an attempt to simplify God. It is to follow the example of great, biblical writers, who through the inspiration of the Holy Spirit, found evidences of God in natural scenes that everyone could perceive. The idea that God is love becomes real to each person when His love for us is described as a father's love, or when we read the story of His Son sacrificing His life for us. John says, "This is how we've come to understand and experience love; Christ sacrificed his life for us." But that abstract concept is made plain when he adds, "if you see some brother or sister in need and have the means to do something about it but turn a cold shoulder.... What happens to God's love? It disappears (1 John 3:16-18 The Message). If you are concerned about making the ways of God plain, think about the world of abstract art. The concept remains in abstraction even though the artist uses the concrete mediums of paint and brush. An art enthusiast would never know the mind of the artist unless his ideas appear in concrete form.

As a writer, you must also mediate between life experiences and the impressions felt by these experiences. Your voice may be able to express the inaudible feelings of many. Readers will respond with gratitude for someone putting into words what they have felt perhaps for many years.

A GRACEFUL VOICE

Your voice, as a Christian writer, will be unique to your style but it should always be dripping with grace. Grace is not to be mistaken for weakness. A graceful voice can be as stern as a Grandmother's ruler. Wisdom will guide you as you learn to clothe a strong voice in the guises of gentleness. A graceful voice allows your message to be heard by a greater number of people and enables you to speak the truth in love. A simple characteristic but one of relevant importance.

AN INSPIRED WORDSMITH

Finally, a distinct feature of a Christian writer is the mark of inspiration. This is what makes our work different than the multitude of others. We are following a calling of God, carefully crafting words to dispense His message. God is our muse as He weaves themes and experiences within our lives supplying all of the material we could ever wish to write about. Do not be burdened by this characteristic. As God has called you, He will travel with you. He will make clear His redemptive heart with the spring of fresh flowers and the budding of new leaves. God has wrapped His words with power, the power to soften hearts, spur revivals, seed revolutions. His Spirit guides you as you open your heart to Him.

WHO ARE YOU NOW

Your true self-identity as a Christian writer is not found in your occupation, whether the collar you wear is white, blue or clerical. Whether you write as a full-time job or during stolen moments in the early morning or middle of the night. It is not even found in your writing itself. Not even in its acceptance or critique. No, your satisfaction of self is found in friendship with the Almighty God. Stripped of all your strivings, you stand as a beloved child of God. Let your writing flow from this reality.

And as you walk the path of a writer, stroll hand in hand with Truth, dropping seeds of hope wherever you go. Keep a keen eye for the many ways God reveals Himself. Speak with a gentle voice that has the strength to carry your message of grace into hostile places. Most of all, be inspired. This is your calling.

INSPIRATION FOR WRITING

———————— Norman G. Wilson ————————

I wrote because God filled me so full I could not help it. He showed me the great center and mainspring of a holy life in Christ crowned within without a rival. That thought took possession of me. I thought on it, preached it, until it finally took the shape of my first book, *Christ Crowned Within*. . . .

—Martin Wells Knapp

Write while the heat is in you. The writer who postpones the recording of his thoughts uses an iron which has cooled to burn a hole with. He cannot inflame the minds of his audience.

— Henry David Thoreau

Writing and reading decrease our sense of isolation. They deepen and widen and expand our sense of life; they feed the soul.

—Anne Lamottt

You can't wait for inspiration. You have to go after it with a club.

— Jack London

You don't write because you want to say something, you write because you've got something to say.

— F. Scott Fitzgerald

I'm a writer as rarely as possible, when forced by an idea too lovely to let die unwritten.

—Richard Bach

Write, therefore, what you have seen, what is now and what will take place later.

—Revelation 1:18–19

4

THE DISCIPLINES OF A CHRISTIAN WRITER

James N. Watkins

*Writing is the hardest way of earning a living, with the
possible exception of wrestling alligators.*

—Olin Miller

I proudly taught this chapter at a writers' conference in 1984 as "How to Succeed as a Christian Writer." However, after my second book's publisher went bankrupt, I started calling my workshop "How to Survive as a Christian Writer." And after my seventh book actually sold negative numbers (more bookstores sent it back than sold it), I was tempted to call it "How to Apply for Government Assistance as a Christian Writer." Writing is hard work, and even after you've signed a book contract and cashed the advance, it doesn't get any easier. It still hasn't for me—even after my twenty-first book project.

So, how does one succeed, or simply survive, as a Christian writer? I think, to paraphrase Stephen Covey, there are seven habits of the highly effective Christian writer.

SELF-DISCIPLINE

Freelancing can easily become free*loading*. It's easier to be raiding the refrigerator than researching; watching *Guiding Light* rather than waiting for

God's guiding light; taking time to relax than taking time to rewrite. I know. I gained ten pounds my first year of freelance writing.

Here are some ways I've found I can discipline myself.

SET A TIME ASIDE EACH DAY FOR WRITING

If you're waiting to find time to write, you will never find it. There's always someone or something else demanding your attention and your time.

Roxanne Armes, my editorial assistant when I worked at Wesleyan Publishing House, was always reminding her co-workers, "You can accomplish anything if you just work on it fifteen minutes a day." She's right. Rhonda Rhea is the author of three books, a busy speaker, and a radio personality as well as a pastor's wife and the mother of five children. How does she do it?

I think the secret is subtracting the fruitless activities from the equation. I've had to learn, for instance, that my TV has to stay off during the day. OK, maybe I still squeeze in an episode of *Murder She Wrote* over lunch, but who can resist Jessica Fletcher? Too much online chatter, too many trips to the mall, too much time playing computer games, too many thousands of holes of golf—most of us have sneaky time-suckers lurking in our routine. I hit a writing roadblock last week (on deadline day, of course) and found myself hiding from the deadline by playing who-knows-how-many mindless games of Minesweeper. How fruitlessly time-sucking is that?

So, view it as a job. (You don't play Minesweeper at work, do you?) Unless you're on life-support, you can write. After double-hernia surgery, I finished a book project with two ice packs down my pants. So, other than life or death situations, there's no real reason not to show up for work.

Four Ds will free up immense chunks of time.

Don't. It's okay to say no to those things that don't contribute to your work assignment from God. For instance, my mission statement is "To communicate the gospel of Christ in as effective and creative manner as possible with as many people as possible."

Cut out those activities that "don't" contribute to your mission statement. *Delegate.* If someone else can do it, he or she should do it. Children can learn to clean, do laundry, fix meals—amazing things. If you have more money than time, hire someone to do things that aren't a part of your mission.

Delay. If you have to do it and no one else will, delay action. Many times circumstances will arise that negate the necessity to do it. I've had a couple conferences, where I was supposed to speak, cancelled by snowstorms and other "acts of God," so I don't start working on a lecture until the point I know I can adequately complete the assignment. And, of course, Jesus could return before your deadline.

Delaying also gives your subconscious or muse (or voices in your head) time to work. I write a weekly column for three papers and a column for each issue of *Rev.* magazine. Weeks before the deadline, my muse (or is it the voices in my head?) starts pitching ideas. I politely tell them to come back a week before my deadline. So, when it's time to start writing, my muse has all kinds of ideas that have germinated in that incubation stage.

Do. If you absolutely have to do it, can't find someone else to do it, and the deadline is approaching, then do it. But not until you've exhausted all your options.

SET DEADLINES FOR YOURSELF

If you don't have an editor breathing down your neck for an assigned article or book project deadline, it's often difficult to get motivated. If you're just starting out in writing, you'll need to be sending out query letters or book proposals, and then waiting for months to hear from an editor. So, there's not a lot of motivation to just do it.

Setting deadlines (if you pass this "line" you're "dead") for yourself, helps to get you going. And reward yourself each time you meet your deadline. Dark chocolate is a power motivator!

SELF-MOTIVATION

Can you *not* write? If it's possible for you not to write, you'll do better as an underwater welder or heavy equipment operator. Real writers, particularly the ones who get published, cannot *not* write. We pitiful, pathetic people with pens are like the prophet Jeremiah who lamented, God's "word is in my heart like a fire, a fire shut up in my bones. I am weary of holding it in; indeed, I cannot" (Jer. 20:9).

If I go more than a few days without writing, I too feel I'm going to be the first documented case of human spontaneous combustion. I cannot *not* write!

Even more than self-motivation, our true motivation must come from beyond ourselves. We must be motivated by a sense of divine call.

SET GOALS

Realistic, specific, and measurable goals will keep you motivated.

Make sure your goals are realistic. Selling more books than Jerry Jenkins and Max Lucado combined is not realistic. Sending out one query letter a month to a magazine is realistic. Finishing the sample chapters for your novel in the next three months is realistic.

Goals also need to be specific. "Becoming a better writer" isn't a specific goal. Finishing this book, subscribing to *The Christian Communicator*, taking a class at the community college, or joining a critique group is specific.

Finally, are your goals measurable? Will you know when you accomplish them?

My agent, Janet Grant, advises writers to "make sure the goal is within your power to accomplish." Getting your book published isn't. One quick "war story:" Tuesday, April 20, 1999, brought news of the horrific killings at Columbine High School in Colorado. Two days later my book proposal, *Dying to Know: Teens' Questions about Death and the Afterlife*, went to the publication board at a major Christian publishing house. The marketing people's response, "Teens aren't interested in death." HUH?

Publication is not in your power. Submitting the best possible proposal with the best possible sample chapters is.

SELF-ORGANIZATION

Here's a test: Can you find your tax return from five years ago within one minute? How 'bout the top of your desk? Freelance writing demands that you keep good financial records, records of where you have sent your manuscripts, and that you keep track of multiple deadlines, etc. (Now where are those tax returns?)

CREATE YOUR WORK ENVIRONMENT

Working off the kitchen table just doesn't work. You'll need a space dedicated to your writing to stay organized. It doesn't have to be an entire room. I started out in a walk-in closet, but I had everything I needed: a computer, printer, phone, file cabinet, and lots of shelving.

Having a space dedicated to writing also helps with self-motivation. If you consistently sit at your desk at the appointed time, your brain will begin to build a strong association with that location and writing. Your subconscious or muse or voices in your head will think, "Hey, she's sitting at her desk, so we better get busy!" After thirty years of sitting in front of a keyboard, I don't have any trouble getting "inspired" to write.

There are also tax advantages to having a percentage of your house as a home office dedicated exclusively to your business. You can deduct that percentage from the mortgage, utilities, insurance, etc. (Talk to a certified tax consultant about the many advantages to having a home office.)

SELF-WORTH

For the first few years of my so-called writing career, my sense of identity and self-worth was wrapped up in being a writer and speaker. So an SASE (self-addressed stamped envelope with a publisher's response to a query) had a direct effect on my SELF-worth. Thin SASEs were usually a check; fat SASEs were my manuscript coming back with the dreaded, "We're sorry but your manuscript does not fit our editorial needs at this time."

It wasn't until I allowed the truth of Brennan Manning's book *Abba's Child* to sink in and "think in" that I broke the grip of "mail domination." I am loved by the Creator of the universe. I am his beloved child. No publisher or conference audience is ever going to love me like God loves me. And there aren't enough rejection slips in Colorado Springs to keep God from loving me.

Sure, rejection still hurts surface emotions, but it no longer cuts to the very heart and soul of Jim Watkins. Jim Watkins is a child of God. Oh, I almost forgot—he also writes books and speaks at conferences.

SELF-PROMOTION

I absolutely cringe at the idea of promoting myself, but it's absolutely crucial. I've finally come to peace with it, realizing that without m-e there is no m-e-s-s-a-g-e. God always sent a messenger with his message—no writing in the sky, but a person. If I don't promote me, the message won't be promoted—and published.

USE PULL RATHER THAN PUSH

Try to push a rope any distance and it will curl up on the ground like a snake. But pull a rope, and it can travel as far as you go. As writers, we won't get far pushing ourselves, but if we can find people to pull us, we can go far. Ask, whom do I know who has "pull"?

For instance, my Campus Life director in high school went on to be the president of Youth for Christ. So, I asked him to write a foreword for one of my books. He also wrote a glowing endorsement for my speaking ministry.

I met Calvin Miller while we were both speaking at a writers' conference. He gladly "pulled" me with a great endorsement. "Jim is one in a million. Two in a million would be overkill." (I think that was an endorsement.)

The reason you bought this book may have been seeing a popular author's name on the cover. They are all people that I have worked with at writers' conferences and were glad to "pull" this book.

PROMOTE THE MESSAGE

Again, remember that you are promoting the message God has given you, not yourself. So shamelessly promote yourself with a Web site, news releases, radio interviews, etc. Carmen Leal's book, *You Can Market Your Book*, is a must read on this subject.

SELF-IMPROVEMENT

We must always be learning to keep our writing edge: subscribe to writers' magazines, attend conferences, take a class at your community college, or sign up for a course with the Christian Writers Guild. Just keep growing. If you're pleased with what you wrote a year ago, you haven't grown as a writer for an entire year!

OTHER-ORIENTATION

Writing is not completely *self*-oriented. You need a support group to keep you disciplined and organized. ("Hi! I'm Jim, and I'm hooked on phonics.") Join a writers' group, ask your friends at church for prayer for your projects (then celebrate together when a check or contract arrives), and keep your spouse or closest friend in the loop.

And network, network, network. Even in Christian publishing, it's *who* you know, not *what* you know that gets your foot in the publishing house door. Build a network of editors and other professional writers as you attend conferences and seminars.

DAVID AND THE
GIANT PUBLISHERS

——————— James N. Watkins ———————

N ow the Publishers gathered together their editors from the far reaches of
the country and were gathered together in the land of the Hoosiers at the
Christian Writers' Workshop. And there were also gathered there writers
from throughout the region. And the editors stood on one side and the writers
were gathered together on the other side, and, behold, there was a great gulf
between them.

And there went out great editors from the camp of the Publishers, who
stood tall in the eyes of the writers. And the editors bore upon themselves
weighty and impressive titles and they were armed with powerful contracts
and, yea, even rejection slips. And their pens were like weavers' beams,
weighing heavy upon the writers' manuscripts.

And the editors came forth as one and called out from the panel to the
writers, "Come forth and send us your manuscripts, for are we not editors and
you not writers? Send forth thine manuscripts, and if they shall overcome our
editorial committees, we shall serve thee with a contract. But, if they shall not,
then thou shalt receive thine SASE in return."

And when the writers and those gathered with them heard these words of
the Publishers, verily they were dismayed and greatly afraid.

Now David, a young writer from Bethlehem, Pennsylvania, who had the
anointing of the Lord upon his head, heard these sayings, and spake to those
about him saying, "What are thou submitting to the Publishers that encamp about
us? For behold, I have brought forth a proposal that the Lord hath given me."

And the people answered after this manner saying, "These editors are great
and powerful, and we are but struggling writers. The battle is too great for us."

And David's older brother, Elieab, heard what he spoke unto those at his
table, and Elieab's anger was kindled against David. Elieab sayeth, "Why
comest thou down hither? And with whom hast thou left thy minimum-wage

job in the steel mill? I know thy pride, and the haughtiness of thy heart; for thou art come down that thou mightest see the Publishers."

And David saith to those at his table, "Thy servant shall present an editor with a proposal, a table of contents, chapter summaries, and three sample chapters."

And those at the table saith as one to him, "Thou art not able to go up to the Publishers, for thou art but a youth, and they have been editing from their youth."

And David saith unto them, "Thy servant has been faithful in attending writers' conferences, in subscribing to the Writer's Digest Book Club, and in journeying unto night classes. And I went forth and did sell short stories and devotionals unto take-home papers and denominational magazines for three cents per word. Behold, I have a portfolio of published work, with which I shall go out to the Publishers.

David moreover said, "The Lord hath caused thine servant to be published in smaller markets; He will deliver my manuscripts into the hands of these great Publishers. And they said unto David, "Go, and the Lord be with thee." But gazing upon his proposal, those sitting at the table saith unto him, thou canst go unto the Publishers. Thou must write this again, in our image and in our style. For behold, no Publisher doth bring forth what thou hath written.

And they re-wrote David's proposal and sample chapters in their own image, in the style of their own making. But David saith unto them, "I canst go with these revisions, for I have not proved them." And David went forth with his original manuscript.

And behold, in the current edition of *The Christian Writers' Market Guide,* it was written that there was a certain editor who did procure and did purchase and did publish manuscripts of such that David hath written. And he took his proposal in his hand, chose him five well-polished stories from his file, put them in his portfolio, and then drew near to the Publishers.

And it came to pass, when the editor arose, and came and drew nigh to meet David, that David hasted, and ran toward the Publishers to meet the editor. And David put his hand in his portfolio, and took thence the proposal, and struck the editor with a single pitch, so that yea, it sank deep into his mind.

So David's proposal prevailed in the house of the Publisher. Therefore, David taketh his pen and signeth the contract. And the people of Israel and of Judah did arise and did go forth and did buy the words that David did write.

THE CRAFT

5

GENERATING IDEAS

Dennis E. Hensley

My mind overflows like a box of kittens.

—Michael Fraley

I spent two dozen years of my life living as a freelance writer for local, regional, national, and international newspapers and magazines. If I didn't write, I had no money for groceries, heat and electric bills, insurance payments, mortgage and car payments, school tuition, clothes, vacations, or retirement investments. Thus, there was never a time when I could say, "Well, I can't think of anything to write about today, so I guess I'll just take the day off." I had to produce salable copy every day (including weekends and holidays) or starve. As such, I became very, *very* good at finding things to write about.

Actually, once you learn to see article ideas everywhere you look, it turns out there are more ideas than there are hours in which to produce the manuscripts. You have to begin by knowing what readers (and, thus, by default, *editors*) want to read about and will pay money to obtain. So, let's begin there.

It has been my experience that magazine articles fall into three specific categories: (1) the "never-miss" category, which contains articles that can always find a market if they are properly researched and well written; (2) the "fairly safe" category, which covers fascinating topics but is aimed at less generic and more focused audiences; and (3) the "risky" category, in which people write about their hobby horses but find no place to sell their finished articles. Here now is the inside scoop on each category.

NEVER-MISS TOPICS

Lifestyles. People never tire of reading about lifestyles. If you know someone so wealthy that he or she lives in a penthouse and leaves for work each day in a private helicopter, write about that person. Conversely, if you know someone who lives deep in a cave to conserve energy, write about him or her. Readers want to know *why* people choose unique lifestyles and what their lives are like (the good and bad elements). So, whether Donald Trump or a hermit, find an extremist and conduct your interview.

Money. Everyone is interested in money. They want to know how to make it, save it, invest it, earn it, compound it, donate it, splurge it, and conserve it. Get any new angle on money and you'll have a money-making article.

Personal advancement ideas and plans. If you can show better ways to dress for success, manage time, apply for a job, win a scholarship, get a promotion, or invite a neighbor to church, you'll make an article sale.

Individual, family, and group activities. How do you entertain three kids in the backseat of your van during a long road trip? What do you do with the senior citizens' group when everyone comes to your house for an evening of fellowship? How do you keep a group of Cub Scouts or Brownies occupied during a visit to your home? If you know of games, projects, and "ice breakers," share them as articles.

Physical fitness and mental health. New information about dieting, exercising, living longer, looking better, managing stress, and improving one's self-image will always find a reading audience. Locate experts in these areas, interview them, and churn out copy.

Entertainment. People who are on budgets (the elderly, large families, and youth leaders) are always interested in finding an entertaining activity that is easily accessible and inexpensive. If you know of museums, sporting contests, zoos, cultural events, art galleries, science halls, hiking trails, or historical landmarks that can provide hours of fun or education but are not high priced, do a travel article about these places.

FAIRLY SAFE TOPICS

Profiles of famous or interesting people. What made this person successful, goal-oriented, self-sacrificing, and driven? By revealing a successful person's insights on life, readers can gain tips on how to improve their own lives.

Coverage of unusual events. Was there a plane crash, record-breaking stunt, unique fund-raising cause, or birth of sextuplets in your city? Be the first to get information on that event and contact editors about it.

Crime. Aspects of crime have, by necessity, become of great interest to readers. White-collar crime, identity theft, carjackings, school hostage crises, and computer invasions are all criminal phenomena of recent years. People are turning to articles and books to show them how to cope with these problems; so, if you have solutions, write them up!

Educational innovations. Online courses, home schooling, distance learning, seminars and workshops, interactive software, and televised classes are fascinating new ways of learning, but most people need writers like you to show them how to take advantage of these opportunities for growth.

RISKY TOPICS

Heavy essays and long editorials. These were popular in an era before multiplex screens and multi-channeled televisions existed. Today, people want news in sound bites, summaries, and flashing images. If you have a complaint, write a letter to the editor, but don't expect to be paid, and don't make it long.

Highly specialized topics. Even if you are an expert in your field, highly-specialized topics have limited reader appeal. People want articles written in laypeople's language that offer functional advice and pragmatic insights. They want to know what time it is, not how to make a watch.

FINDING THOSE GREAT ARTICLE IDEAS

Okay, now that you know what readers want and editors will buy, let's find out where to go "hunting" for great ideas for articles.

MAXIMIZE LEADS FOUND IN YOUR DAILY NEWSPAPER

Comb the want ads for offbeat services (musket repair shop), bizarre items for sale (fallout shelter equipment), tempting offers (money for blood donations), and unusual events (annual polka festival). With the right "spin," these ads could become feature articles. Likewise, look for small articles that you could enhance for a larger medium. If triplets are getting married in the same wedding ceremony, it might be a filler item in the local paper, but it could be a two-page feature with photos for *Modern Bride* magazine. Likewise, find local events that can be given a regional slant. The opening of a new doll exhibit at your historical museum might rate one photo and a few paragraphs in the local paper, but you could make it a "must see" travel feature for *Midwest Traveler* or *RV and Camper Quarterly*.

SCOUR THE YELLOW PAGES OF YOUR CITY AND AREA PHONEBOOKS

Contact "associations" and "organizations" for news of personnel hiring, promotions, and buyouts. Do feature articles on businesses celebrating their twenty-fifth or fiftieth years in business. Discover unusual businesses and reveal their secrets. (How do they get those fortunes inside fortune cookies without getting them all gushy?) Find new slants on routine businesses, such as florists who provide meat-eating plants to botany and biology classes or army surplus shops that cater to doomsday alarmists. Consider combining two topics, such as pig farming and egg production: "Ham and Eggs—the Breakfast Business!" Each state has thousands of cities, and each city has a phonebook with pages of ads. Mine those ads.

PROBE FACULTY BIOGRAPHIES IN THE BACK OF COLLEGE CATALOGS

You can work this from two angles. If you have a topic you need to write about, scan the listings of credentials until you find an expert on that topic and then call and arrange for an interview with him or her. For example, if you need to write 1,500 words on global population control, find someone in a college sociology department who did a dissertation on that topic or has written monographs or books on the topic. Or, in reverse order, find out what a college professor is an expert in, and then come up with a newsworthy angle on that for an interview feature. For instance, if a professor is an expert on international law, interview her for an article on "War Crime Trials: World War II Germany to Modern Day Iraq."

Professors love getting their names in print. They'll answer all your questions and save you days of research online or in a library.

MAKE KEY CONTACTS WITH "CONNECTED" PEOPLE

If you want great anecdotes, then maintain a running dialogue with people who are in people-service occupations. Get your notebook and tape recorder and make the rounds of teachers, barbers, beauticians, real estate agents, pastors, union leaders, waiters, cab drivers, emergency room physicians, police officers, and politicians. Whether on- or off-the-record, these people can tell you hilarious real-life stories of people's foibles, weird accidents, crazy stunts, silly explanations, oddball letters, bizarre requests, and outrageous senses of logic. From this you can get ideas for short stories, humorous fillers, thoughts for devotions, comedy material for speeches, and round-up articles about off-beat subjects.

MONITOR THE MEDIA

If you want to write for your city newspaper or your area monthly magazines, then break in by localizing national news items. For example, if Agent Orange is thought to be causing cancer in Vietnam War veterans, go to your local Veterans of Foreign War or American Legion halls and interview vets in your city and county who are suffering from this problem. If privatizing Social Security has senior citizens in a national uproar, go to retirement communities in your town and conduct interviews with folks who are supportive of or upset by this trend. Keep in mind that news is only news if it has an impact on your target readers.

So if you have access to a daily newspaper, a telephone book, some college catalogs, and a television set, you have a cornucopia of article ideas presenting themselves to you. Now, the big decision comes next: Which one should you write *first*?

MILK EVERY SALE TO ITS FULL POTENTIAL

Dennis E. Hensley

Too many times, beginning writers get the notion that once an article is written and sold, it is "dead." That's hardly the truth. In reality, one article can go through a life cycle that can result in as many as fifteen to twenty-five separate sales. The key is to retain the rights to your material (don't sell to publications that buy "all rights"), be patient enough to move from small markets to ever-enlarging markets, and to work in a sequential pattern so your article won't appear simultaneously in competing markets. Here's one model to follow in your marketing strategy.

LOCAL NEWSPAPERS

Try to sell your article first to your local newspaper. Focus on news tidbits and key facts that will be of interest to readers in that very narrow readership area.

SHOPPERS AND TABLOIDS

If your county has a once-a-week shopper or district tabloid, sell your article next to this market, but expand the news information to explain ways in which your topic would have broader appeal to a greater readership.

STATEWIDE MAGAZINES AND NEWSPAPERS

Send clippings of your article as it appeared in your local papers, along with a query letter, to the editors of statewide magazines or newspaper Sunday supplements. Make them aware of something happening in your part of the state that would be informative or entertaining to readers throughout the state.

REGIONAL PUBLICATIONS

Attempt to sell your article to regional publications that would not have seen it in *your* state's newspapers and magazines. For example, an article on improving farming techniques in the Midwest will sell just as well in Ohio, Indiana, Illinois, and Kentucky as it may have sold for you in Michigan or Wisconsin. Likewise, an article on deep-sea fishing or whale watching will sell just as well in Maine as it did in Virginia.

SPECIALTY PUBLICATIONS

If your article focuses on a person, then sell the article to any specialty publications that may have a connection to that person (service club, church, veterans' organization, union, college, or political party).

NATIONAL PERIODICALS

Finally, submit the article to general-interest national (and even international) periodicals, always showing the value of the information to the broadest spectrum of readers.

6

LEARNING THE CRAFT

Jerry B. Jenkins

*Beginning writers must appreciate the prerequisites if they hope
to become writers. You pay your dues—which takes years.*

—Alex Haley

Writers read. Re-reading favorites like *Cold Mountain*, *All Over but the Shoutin'*, *In Cold Blood*, and *Stein on Writing* teaches me something new every time. Sometimes I read lines or paragraphs over and over just to savor them. I read everything I can get my hands on. Right now I'm on a campaign to cover classics I missed in my early years.

READ, READ, READ

Become conversant in the bestsellers so you know what people are reading, even if it's not clear why. Keep in mind that Christians are called to be in the world but not of the world, so take care not to get mired in the muck. Your own writing will ring true only if you realistically portray the dark side of life, but a writer with a Christian worldview will always reflect hope. That doesn't mean every story has a happy ending, but it certainly means readers should see vestiges of redemption, forgiveness, sacrifice, . . . and hope.

When it comes to growing in the nuts and bolts of writing, I always recommend the Strunk and White classic, *The Elements of Style*. But that's only a jumping-off point. You should have numerous books on writing on your shelves, and many are widely available.

CORRESPONDENCE COURSES
AND COMMUNITY COLLEGE CLASSES

If you're serious about improving, consider a correspondence course or a college class. My Christian Writers Guild, founded more than forty years ago by Norman B. Rohrer, provides training to authors who want to grow.

We offer a two-year, fifty-lesson Apprentice course designed to strengthen your ability and sharpen your confidence. Unique to our "What's Your Story?" course is our use of personal mentors to push writers past hobby-ism to professionalism. We cover fiction and nonfiction articles and books, along with screenwriting. Our emphasis is on getting writers published in paying markets.

Each lesson builds upon the previous and is evaluated via e-mail by a distinguished veteran writer or editor, recognized in the publishing industry. Among the more than three dozen, they have published thousands of stories, novels, newspaper columns, and magazine articles.

The hallmark of the Guild is that every student is assigned a mentor. Personal tutelage makes all the difference. Many students develop friendships with their mentors during the two years it takes to complete the course.

Succeeding takes work. We expect a one-lesson-every-two-weeks pace. That gives students a sense of how to meet deadlines, to push themselves even when they might rather curl up with the remote control. For details, visit www.ChrsitianWritersGuild.com.

The Guild also offers a Journeyman course for advanced writers and grads of the Apprentice level, and we have created curriculum for young writers as well. Our Pages and Squires courses cover kids from nine to twelve and thirteen and up. Of course we're not the only such option. There's no excuse for not improving one's skills with so many opportunities available.

WRITERS' CONFERENCES

Beyond reading, find outlets to meet other writers. Writers' conferences are a great place to find fellow travelers on the rough road to a contract, to exchange ideas, and to talk out plots. Who else really understands our struggle to find the right word or endure the agony of editing?

You'll not only discover new ways of thinking, but you'll also build a network. Many of my early freelance assignments began with contacts at writers' conferences. One of the best ways to improve the odds against getting published is taking the time and trouble to get to know other writers, swap stories about who's buying, and get access to editors and publishers.

Some of the best conferences include—

- Colorado Christian Writers' Conference, Estes Park, Colorado;
- Mount Hermon Christian Writers' Conference, near San Jose, California;
- Sandy Cove Christian Writers' Conference, North East, Maryland;
- Write to Publish Christian Writers' Conference, Wheaton, Illinois;
- Wesleyan Publishing House's Christian Writers' Workshop, Indianapolis, Indiana;
- Christian Writers Guild's Writing for the Soul conference, Colorado Springs, Colorado.

WRITERS' GROUPS

After a conference, find a writers' group in your area. Find other like-minded authors, including those who have the expertise and experience to make it worthwhile. Find a group where you can be sure the input is valid.

If the participants spend inordinate time whining about how tough it is to get published, that's a red flag. Look elsewhere until you find writers on their way up. If necessary, start a group of your own, recruiting at least one published writer to offer leadership.

BOOK DISCUSSION GROUPS

Consider joining a book discussion group. Check with libraries, bookstores, or online. These groups offer chances to speak your mind and find out what others are thinking—invaluable for one who wants to create real characters and write what people want to read.

A MENTOR

Finally, find a mentor—someone with the time to also offer hands-on instruction. Again, writers' conferences will often lead you to mentor possibilities.

When you find someone willing to give you honest feedback and offer suggestions, be mindful of how precious a gift you've been given. This means respecting your mentor's schedule. He or she will also have writing goals and deadlines, so give him or her space and plenty of time to respond.

Most mentoring can be handled online. You send a writing sample and then wait for the words you most need to hear (though they may sting at first). Respond with an occasional note of appreciation, but don't overdo it. Your mentor wouldn't be spending the time with you unless he believed you worthy of the investment.

It's not enough to have a God-given desire to write. Continually hone your skills and seek every opportunity to grow. Read all you can, build lasting relationships with other writers, find a mentor, and plant yourself in front of that monitor. That's how every blockbuster begins.

IN REVIEW

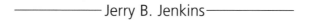

Jerry B. Jenkins

Even loners need to know what people think, how they feel, and what they do. Professionals keep in touch with each other and keep learning.

Create a core of writing books you frequently reference. Keep adding to your collection, and regularly cycle back to refresh yourself on both the fine points and the basics easily forgotten in the fervor to get words on paper.

Attend writers' conferences to build relationships. It's well worth your time and money to pull out of the daily dullness and learn more about your craft. Commiserate and encourage, then keep in touch.

Find a critique group, and develop a thick skin. It's crucial to muster the confidence to submit your work for comment. Beware the blind leading the blind, however. Listen to those you respect, implement what makes sense, and discard the rest.

Finally, find a mentor. You'll grow only if you challenge yourself. The key is to establish a relationship with a veteran author who can both nurture and admonish you. That's how young writers learn and published authors improve.

7

PLANNING YOUR WRITING

Stan Toler

Like stones, words are laborious and unforgiving, and the fitting of them together, like the fitting of stones, demands great patience and strength of purpose and particular skill.

—Edmund Morrison

Writers and architects have much in common. Both create a work out of nothing but imagination and creativity. Both need to follow rules and protocols for solid foundations, firm construction, aesthetic and pleasing design, and customer satisfaction. Let's look at writing an article or book the way an architect and contractor would look at building a house.

UNDERSTAND WHY YOU ARE WRITING THE ARTICLE OR BOOK

Just as the contractor's blueprint begins in the heart and mind of the architect, so articles and books begin in the heart and mind of the writer—freshly touched by the Spirit, recently revived by the Scripture, and newly led by times of prayer and meditation.

Ask yourself, why do I want to write this article or book? For fame and fortune? (Sorry, Christian writing has very little of that.) To set people straight? (Not a God-pleasing motivation.) Or, to use my talents and abilities to help others in their spiritual journey?

KNOW YOUR AUDIENCE

Ask yourself these questions as well.

WHO ARE MY READERS, AND WHAT IS HAPPENING IN THEIR LIVES?

Your writing must fit the demographics of the audience. A story about eight-track audio tapes, for instance, will be met with significant silence if it's written to teenagers more familiar with digital video discs (DVD) and MP3 audio technology. The speaker should always try to communicate to the audience's level of understanding.

WHAT DOES MY AUDIENCE NEED?

Certainly your readers don't need recycled *Reader's Digest* articles or playback versions of some media minister's work. They need a fresh word to invigorate spiritual lives that are often as stale as a six-day-old Krispy Kreme donut.

Finley Peter Dunne, one of the great journalists of the 1900s, wrote that a writer's job is to "comfort the afflicted and to afflict the comfortable." Which do your readers need right now?

WHAT WILL MY AUDIENCE NEED?

Effective communicators listen for the future. On a clear night, you can hear a train coming from far away. The sound is faint at first, almost imperceptible. But a careful listener can hear it. Leaders listen for the train that has not yet arrived. They look for trends that are just over the horizon; their ears are tuned for changes in the economy, the culture, and even in politics. Leaders hear change coming long before it arrives.

HAVE A FLOOR PLAN

There is no mystery to the preparation of a good article or book. As with building a house, there are stages of construction. The builder who follows a plan and stays on schedule will produce a sound structure. It's the same with writing.

I wouldn't hire a builder who arrived at construction sites wondering, "What kind of house should I build today?" I'd want my contractor to do some planning!

DESIGN AN INVITING ENTRYWAY

The lead, or first few paragraphs of an article must grab the attention, first of the editor, and then the reader. Without a strong beginning, the editor will be reaching for a rejection slip, and the reader will be turning the magazine page for something more interesting.

Author and speaker Jim Watkins suggests that a good lead begins with a felt need of the reader. Abraham Maslov notes that people desire safety, security, a sense of belonging, and to make a difference in their world. Engage them on the feeling level: "Are your children fearful following the 9/11 attacks?" "Do you ever feel alone in a church of two thousand?" "Is your prayer life stale and boring?"

Or simply start with a story or a quote, but make sure you can verify its authenticity with at least two sources. (Urban legends discredit you as an author.)

A humorous anecdote is also an effective lead.

TRIM IT WITH FRESH DELIVERY

A house may be framed, enclosed, sided, and roofed, but it's not finished until it's finished (as Yogi Berra might say). Wallboard looks dull without a coat of paint. Corners without trim look rough and incomplete. The "trimmings" give the house warmth.

In the same way, articles, books, and sermons need to be finished with a fresh delivery. Even the most profound thoughts look dull without a little dressing up.

Jesus talked about seasoning your speech with salt. Could it be that the one who mentioned camels going through the eyes of needles and compared religious hypocrites to painted walls was recommending a smattering of light application along with the heavy principles of timeless truth?

I have seen a well-placed story almost instantly seal the truth I had been struggling to communicate. Through the years, my preaching, teaching, and writing endeavors have always included humor. I believe it's a wonderful way to gain attention, put people at ease, hold interest, and clarify truth.

INCLUDE ILLUSTRATIONS TO LET IN LIGHT

A house with no windows would be dreary. A good architect uses light effectively to set the mood for each room.

The "windows" in writing are quotations, humor, and other material that adds interest to your subject. A wise writer is constantly on the lookout for illustrations. Scan the newspaper. Subscribe to good magazines. Notice what's popular on television and in film. Jot down observations. Surf the Net.

When you find good material, file it. Be good to your files, and they'll be good to you. However, before using an illustration, make sure you feel good about it. If it doesn't make sense to you, and if you don't feel good about it, it probably will be received like an ugly cousin's kiss.

The placement of illustrations, like the design of lighting, is more art than science. Experience teaches when to use humor or drama, quotes or statistics, poetry or anecdotes. A capable communicator will use each in its proper place. These are the doors and windows that let light travel back and forth in the building.

SUBMIT YOUR WORK TO A GOOD INSPECTOR

The story is told of a man who bought his first boat. It was shiny, new, powerful, and expensive. He couldn't wait to launch it and show it off to his friends. But no matter how hard he tried, the boat just wouldn't respond. It was sluggish. It wouldn't plane. He just couldn't maneuver it. He began to look around the boat and to check everything topside. Everything seemed to be working

Seeing his plight, the mechanic from a nearby marina motored out to him. Soon the mechanic was in the water checking underneath the boat, trying to find the problem. Immediately he surfaced and said to the new boat owner: "I think I've spotted the problem. We recommend you take the boat off the trailer before you put it in the water!"

Editors, like building inspectors (and marina mechanics), can help us see the dangerous defects in our work.

Don't forget the details. They will make all the difference in the world to your presentation.

Ask a friend to read your piece—critically. Join a writers' critique group (you can find groups by contacting your local library).

Although a contractor has delivered a house to the buyer, the work may not be completed. There may be some post-sale details to care for, a nail or two that wasn't quite right, or a minor repair that is needed. A good builder will follow up on those details.

The secret to good writing is rewriting!

COVER IT WITH PRAYER

The roof is the least noticeable feature on most houses, but the most important. Every builder knows that a bad roof will spoil a good house. The roof is the shelter. The roof on your writing is prayer.

At this moment, the article or book is a good collection of words on paper. But they won't impact your people without the power of the Holy Spirit.

TOLER'S TIPS FOR AUTHORS

Stan Toler

1. Practice writing something daily.
2. Write like you talk.
3. Use all five senses in telling a story.
4. Create a file on every book idea.
5. Understand why you are writing the book.
6. Know your audience.
7. Brainstorm your book plans with a trusted friend.
8. Ask for input and constructive criticism.
9. Check out the competition for your book ideas.
10. Read widely and research diligently.
11. Outline the entire project before you begin writing.
12. Communicate out of the wealth of your personal experience.
13. Read good fiction to get the creativity flowing.
14. Seek out good editors to proofread your work.
15. Brace yourself for rejection.

8

BASIC GRAMMAR
AND WHY IT MATTERS

Dennis E. Hensley

*Ignorant people think it is the noise which fighting cats make
that is so aggravating, but it ain't so; it is the sickening
grammar that they use.*

—Mark Twain

Years ago a highly successful novelist and playwright used to walk around with a dictionary under his arm. Sometimes people would stop him and ask, "Why do you carry that dictionary everywhere you go?" The author would shrug his shoulders, smile and admit, "Because I don't know all the words yet."

I like that story. As writers, we need to carry the tools of our trade around with us the same way a physician carries a leather satchel with scalpels, bandages, and thermometers or a mechanic carries a toolbox with wrenches, hammers, and screwdrivers. We need to be "equipped" with an expanded vocabulary, a solid knowledge of proper grammar and punctuation, a sharp eye for correct spelling, and a trained ear for smooth transitions and natural syntax.

That is especially true today. In bygone eras when computers and MP3 players and cell phones and e-zines and fax machines didn't exist, life moved at a slower pace. In those days editors could send manuscripts back for a second, third, or even fourth rewrite. Today, editors want manuscripts to come in fast, they want them to come in accurate, and they want them to come in ready for distribution. That means you have to be your own copyeditor and proofreader. And you'd better be good at both tasks if you expect to compete in the major markets.

I've spent several decades as a writing coach and university writing professor. Obviously, I cannot review in one brief chapter all the rules of writing. As such, let me recommend that you consider buying and studying such books as *Teach Yourself Grammar and Style in 24 Hours* by Pamela Rice Hahn and Dennis E. Hensley, *The New American Dictionary of Good English* by Norman Lewis, or a current edition of *The MLA Handbook* published by the Modern Language Association. Having made these recommendations for later study, let me now point out to you some specific ways in which you can sharpen the mechanics of your writing (while also warning you about some of the most common errors writers commit).

PROPER USE OF ITALICS

Italic type slants to the right and is used by writers and editors either to indicate some sort of emphasis or to highlight reference tools. For example, the italicized word in this sentence would be emphasized: "You're talking to me as though I'd gone *crazy*!" Italics are also used for the titles of reference materials such as books, magazines, plays, catalogs, or movies, as in, "Did you watch *Anne of Green Gables* last night?" or "I renewed my subscription to *Advanced Christian Writer*." Some editors like to use italics for foreign words (*quid pro quo*) or abbreviated titles, as in, "Each time I read Margaret Mitchell's *GWTW*, I come away wishing she'd written a second novel" (for *Gone with the Wind*).

Warning: In pre-word processor days, writers used to underline words to indicate italics to a typesetter. Never use underlining and italics together, since they mean the same thing.

PROPER USE OF PARENTHESES

Parentheses are the curved punctuation marks that are used to enclose a parenthetical expression (such as an amplifying or explanatory word or phrase), to enclose part of a sentence not directly related to the main part (such as mentioning that I'm writing this in early evening), to enclose an appositive (one of my favorite words in highbrow English) phrase, or to present explanatory words after a phase such as *cum grano salis* (with a grain of salt). They can also be used as part of mathematical equations (a + b) or to clarify where a place like Millerton (Texas) is or to provide alternate explanations of such numbers as three hundred dollars ($300.00). They can be used in such lists as (1) your car keys, (2) your briefcase, and (3) your topcoat. Warning: Place end punctuation inside the parentheses only if an entire sentence is inside it. If a comma, period, semicolon, or exclamation point is part of the sentence, it goes after the closing parenthesis. Using half of a parentheses is improper writing, such as, "Dave said I could have the option of 1) renting an apartment or 2) living in the dormitory."

PROPER USE OF BRACKETS

Brackets are the two square-ended punctuation marks. They can be used to insert personal commentary or missing words inside a quotation, as in, "Sure, we like [and would endorse] Dianna Jenkins for state senator." They also can delineate when one set of parenthetical words appears inside a larger set of parentheses, as in this example: (Marge told me [and no one else] what the safe's combination was.)

Warning: Do not get into the habit of using brackets randomly, such as explaining something that is already obvious or something that can be understood from the context of the sentence.

PROPER USE OF QUOTATION MARKS

Although quotation marks are used most often to indicate quotations (direct quotes and dialogue), they also serve other functions. For the exact words of a speaker, the quotation marks frame the words spoken, as in, "I'll be at work early," said Charlie, "if there is no traffic jam." If a paraphrasing of someone's words is offered, put only the person's exact words in quotations marks: Margie announced there would be five winners, so be sure to "hold your door prize tickets."

Poems and song titles are put inside quotation marks, as are the titles of chapters in books, lectures, sermons, pamphlets, short stories, handbooks, and newspaper and magazine articles. Use quotation marks to draw attention to key words you wish to define in the rest of your sentence: Restrooms are called "the head" by Marines and referred to as "latrines" by soldiers. If medical, engineering, or scientific terms cannot be substituted for layperson's language, put those words inside quotations marks: Doctors believe that "progeria" may cause children to age seven times faster than normal growth rates.

If you quote a full stanza from a poem or song, put quotation marks before the first line and at the end of the last line.

Warning: If you write for British, Canadian, or any other foreign publishers who use British punctuation, there will be changes in placement of the quotation marks. In American usage, commas and periods go inside the quotation marks, but for the British they go outside. Suggestion: To understand British punctuation, read *Eats, Shoots & Leaves: The Zero Tolerance Approach to Punctuation* by Lynne Truss.

PROPER USE OF THE COMMA

Whole books could be written about the proper use of the comma, but for space considerations let me focus on its six most common uses.

1. Short word units that interrupt the common structure of a sentence are called "parenthetical expressions." They should be set off by commas.

Example: Your claim, I'm afraid, was filed after the nine-month time limitation and, thus, cannot be honored.

2. "Exclamatory words" that come at the start of a sentence are set off by a comma.

Examples: Well, at long last I have an answer for you. Yes, we did receive your letter last Tuesday!

3. Whenever a sentence addresses someone personally, it uses a comma to set off the "personal address" word(s).

Example: Your account is two months past due, Mrs. Lake.

Example: Therefore, my old pal, I will be at your retirement banquet tonight.

4. "Items in a series" are set off by commas, including a comma before the coordinating conjunction *and* if it makes the meaning of the sentence clearer.

Example: My favorite sandwiches are tuna fish, grilled cheese, and peanut butter.

By inserting a comma before *and*, it clarifies that the grilled cheese and the peanut butter are separate sandwiches.

5. Use commas to set off "dependent clauses" (phrases that cannot stand alone) in a sentence.

Example: If you can work on Friday, I'll schedule you for overtime.

6. An appositive is a word or group of words used to give clarifying information about the noun or pronoun in front of it.

Example: The owner of Tennessee Repair Company, Mr. Andrew Delmar, has suggested a salvage value of fifty dollars for the broken lamp.

Example: I called Donna Jean Sumner, the new van line's agent in Detroit, to inquire about your missing golf bag.

AVOIDING SEXIST LANGUAGE

Whereas mechanics are very important in professional writing, so are word choices. Naturally, one can overdo it when trying to be "politically correct" and "nonsexist," but some element of sensitivity is warranted in this area.

By using plurals, you can avoid awkward gender pronouns.

Bad example: When a surgeon operates, he/she uses a scalpel.

Good example: When surgeons operate, they use a scalpel.

Here are some words to be aware of, as well as some acceptable alternate words:

Actor/actress: actor, performer, movie star
Cameraman: photographer, camera operator
Chairman: department chair, director, supervisor
Fireman, policeman: firefighter, police officer
Man-hours: work-hours, set routine, established work shift
Mankind: people, civilization, folks, humanity
Manmade: handmade, synthetic, tooled items, artificial
Manpower: staff, crew, employees, personnel, workers
Mailman: letter carrier, postal worker
Night watchman: security officer, gate guard

Waiter/waitress: server

Steward/stewardess: flight attendant, cabin staff

IMPROVING YOUR ABILITY TO PROOFREAD

Have you ever heard the story of how a government executive once wasted four million dollars by not catching a hyphen error when proofreading a business letter? In originally dictating his letter to his secretary, the executive said, "We want 100-foot-long radium bars for our reactor. Send three in cases." The secretary misunderstood what he was saying and later typed, "We want 100 foot-long radium bars." Two months later the government agency received three huge crates containing 100 ruler-sized, cut-down, totally useless radium bars.

Here are some tips to help prevent you from ever making embarrassing typographical, statistical, and stylistic errors.

READ YOUR MANUSCRIPT ALOUD

Reading something audibly helps you gauge its rhythm, pace, sound, and degree of difficulty. If you discover that certain passages cause you to be tongue-tied or seem long-winded, rewrite them in more simplified language. Use simple declarative sentences. Keep your paragraphs short. Strive for clarity and power.

READ BACKWARD

If you read sentences in the same sequence you wrote them, you may read into the sentences things that might not really be there. Since you already know what your article or story is supposed to say, you may anticipate "ghost" words. To guarantee that you do see each word, try reading backward from the last word on a page to the first word. By doing this, you'll notice if a word is misspelled, if a period has been left out of an abbreviation, or if a capital letter has been overlooked. Keep in mind that computer spellcheckers cannot discern whether you meant to type *rain, reign,* or *rein,* or if you meant to type *sew, sow,* or *so*.

SHUFFLE PAGES

As long as the pages of a twenty-page short story or book chapter are numbered, there is no reason you cannot shuffle them. Each page can then be analyzed as one unit, and you will not be distracted by your concentration on the overall content.

LET IT REST

If possible, let your rough drafts or page proofs rest in a desk drawer a few days. Later, you can proofread the copy with "new eyes." You will have forgotten the exact sequence you originally used in the written version, and you will now be able to serve as a more unbiased reader. (Years after high school graduation, have you ever come across some of your old theme papers? If only you could have judged them *then* with the cold eye of time you have *now*. The same principle applies to your current writing projects. So, let them sit and get "old and cold.")

VARY THE ROUTINE

If you get a huge stack of galleys of your forthcoming book, do not overload your senses by trying to blitz through the pages in one sitting. Vary the routine by reading and editing just two or three chapters. Then set the rest aside and watch TV, do some writing, or clean your office. Hours later, or perhaps the next day, come back and do another three chapters. Keep alert and fresh when proofreading.

SEEK HELPERS

If someone at your writers' club needs help on a project, work out a barter deal in which you will copyedit her manuscript if she will proofread your galleys. If you have a secretary or spouse or older child who would be willing to serve as a second set of eyes, enlist that person to help with the proofreading of your manuscripts. When it comes to proofreading pages, two heads really are better than one.

HIRE PROFESSIONALS

If you feel you have done the best job you can on getting your manuscript ready to submit to a publisher, but you have some confidence issues with your ability to spot all grammar or punctuation or spelling mistakes, consider hiring a professional editor. Some high school and college English teachers will moonlight as proofreaders. Lists of editorial services are listed in *Sally Stuart's Christian Writers' Market Guide* and in *Writer's Market*. Often, when you get your marked-up copy back in the mail from a professional editor, not only will the manuscript now be flawless, but you will also be able to see mistakes you are making and learn how not to repeat them in the future.

SUMMARY

How important are the mechanics of writing? Well, you would not go to a job interview without making sure that you were dressed appropriately and well groomed. Similarly, it would be equally unprofessional to send a manuscript to an editor if it was not pristine in appearance. This means that grammar, syntax, punctuation, format, style, transitions, and spelling need to be flawless. Don't have a "mechanical breakdown."

Editor's note: Book publishers tend to use *The Chicago Manual of Style* for their guide to grammar, punctuation, and style; newspapers and online publications tend to use *The Associated Press Stylebook and Libel Manual*.

WAYS TO TRIM THE DEADWOOD FROM YOUR MANUSCRIPTS

—————— Dennis E. Hensley ——————

A s you read over your first drafts, start slashing anything that does not bear fruit, i.e. deadwood. Here are some ways to go about it.

CUT OUT WORDY DELAYING OF THE SUBJECT

Note in these examples how the italicized words can be deleted from the sentences without losing any of the meaning.

Example: *There are* many students *who* should not be in college.

Example: *It happens that* I've known about this for two years.

CONDENSE WORDY PHRASING

Notice in the examples below that many words can be condensed into one or two words without changing the meaning.

Example: He spoke to me *concerning the matter of* my future. (Use *about*.)

Example: *My field of employment is that of teaching.* (Rewrite as *I teach*.)

USE PRECISION WORDS

A carefully used verb, adverb, or adjective can do the work of a lengthy clause or phrase, as evidenced in these examples.

Example: The wind which blew through the cracks made a whistling sound.

Strong Verb: The wind *whistled* through the cracks. (This eliminates five words.)

Example: He walked down the street as if he had a purpose.

Strong Adverb: He walked *purposefully* down the street. (This eliminates six words.)

Example: She told a story that no one could believe.

Strong Adjective: She told an *unbelievable* story. (This eliminates five words.)

ELIMINATE REDUNDANCIES

By using basic logic, you will often see that some words you have inserted into your sentences do nothing but state the obvious. Here are some examples of redundant statements: large *in size*; red *in color*; biography *of her life*; repeat *again*; continue *on*; return *back*; recur *again*; sunset *in the west*; *very* unique; changed places *with each other*; I thought *to myself*; round *in shape*; necessary *requisites*; *resultant* effect; and *important* essential.

WHENEVER POSSIBLE, USE SHORTER WORDS AND FEWER WORDS

Nobody is impressed with multi-syllabic or multitudinous words. (See my point?) So, compress and reduce. Here are some good examples: extensive conflagration (big fire); higher institution of learning (college); a substantial segment of the population (many people); rejoined in the negative (said no); discharged his financial obligation (paid).

9

WRITING DEVOTIONALS

Ron McClung

*Writing became such a process of discovery that I couldn't
wait to get to work in the morning: I wanted to know
what I was going to say.*

—Sharon O'Brien

I became fascinated with devotional writing in college. One of my professors showed me a copy of a church newsletter in which the pastor regularly wrote a devotional article. It was impressive to me that the pastor said something significant, said it well, and said it succinctly.

Later I worked at a church where the senior pastor regularly wrote a short devotional article for the newsletter. When he went on vacation, it became my responsibility to pinch-hit for him, including the creation of the article. I took it seriously and worked hard on the assignment. Like most writers, it gave me a warm feeling to put my thoughts on paper and then see them come to life on the printed page. Never mind that it was only a few hundred copies; I was in print! As C. S. Lewis said, "It is sown in inky scratches, it is raised in print." Just enough positive response came my way to encourage me to keep writing positive, inspirational articles.

Years later the idea surfaced to write an article for the local newspaper during Advent. I presented the idea to the religion editor, emphasizing my goals of keeping it short—four hundred words or less, positive, and aimed at people who didn't normally read the church page. She agreed to let me try it for four weeks. After the Advent season I proposed continuing the articles on a weekly basis. Again she agreed. That was more than seventeen years and nearly nine hundred articles ago.

There are several different types of devotional articles, based on the starting point of each one. Let's look at four types.

SCRIPTURE VERSE OR PASSAGE

A common way to begin is with a Scripture verse or passage. An invitation to write for our denominational devotional booklet includes an assigned Scripture passage, but the writer chooses a verse to emphasize. The writer tries to make that verse come alive in some contemporary application, usually in 250 words or less.

RELEVANT THEME

A second beginning point is a relevant theme. For instance, holidays provide inspiration for some articles. In seventeen years, I have written nearly seventy Advent articles for the newspaper. Easter, Mother's Day, Valentine's Day, Thanksgiving, and other holidays provide a peg upon which to hang my written thoughts. Current events may stimulate articles that connect with what people are already thinking. The anniversary of some historical event, although not necessarily a holiday, may also provide a springboard for some devotional thoughts.

WRITER'S OWN READING

Third, the writer's own reading may inspire an article. A statement in a magazine, a pithy quotation from a book, or an article in the newspaper may trigger ideas that result in devotional pieces.

LIFE EXPERIENCES

Life experiences supply a fourth source of inspiration for devotional articles. In recent years, my job has taken my wife and me to various places around the United States and Canada. Mission trips have provided exposure to Europe and Asia. The people we meet, the sights we see, and the experiences we have all stimulate the creative juices, and devotional articles are often the result.

What makes it a devotional article rather than a travelogue piece or an observation on culture? What causes it to inspire rather than simply inform? When one starts with Scripture, the devotional element is somewhat built in. But when starting with life experience or a particular theme, the writer must purposely guide the reader's thoughts to a relevant Scripture verse, a characteristic of God, an inspiring biblical promise, or some other uplifting idea. How does one do this?

The short answer is to practice! A life spent studying the Bible is an asset. Encountering an interesting person may remind the writer of a Bible character, and the writer can draw a comparison between the two. An experience or event may bring to mind a familiar passage of Scripture. At other times, no Scripture comes to mind. That's when I pull out my trusty concordance, look up a word or a topic, and find an appropriate Scripture. The danger here lies in finding a Scripture that seems to fit and taking it out of context, forcing it to say something the original biblical writer did not intend. On the other hand, it is amazing that Scripture so thoroughly addresses the human condition, cutting across boundaries of age, culture, race, and lifestyle.

Another way to look at devotional writing is to think in terms of one's purpose. Are you writing to inform, inspire, entertain, challenge, or convict? All those purposes are legitimate for devotional pieces, except perhaps the latter, since convicting people is really the Holy Spirit's job (see John 16:8). When we try too hard to do it with our writing, we come across as "preachy" and judgmental. The truth itself is convicting, so if our writing has the ring of authenticity, it will convict when necessary. The best devotionals are those that challenge but do it in an inspirational way. One popular devotional book carries the sub-title, "Spirit-Lifting Thoughts for Every Day of the Year." A worthy goal is to lift the spirit of the reader.

Knowing your intended audience will have a bearing on how you write devotionally. When I began writing for the newspaper, I imagined a person who did not usually read the church page. He or she would be leafing through the newspaper and would be attracted by a title or the first few words of an article. So I typically began my column with some non-religious theme, event, or observation. I assumed that most readers were not very familiar with the Bible. Yet before the article was finished, I would relate it to a biblical verse or concept that would direct the reader toward God. My goal was also to keep the article short enough that by the time the reader decided whether to read the whole piece, he or she had finished it.

When writing for a devotional booklet, I know the audience will consist primarily of Christians, so I am not confined by my non-religious launching pad. I can move more quickly to biblical themes.

Be sure your article makes a point. Even if you are expounding on a verse of Scripture, if you can make a single point in a short article instead of trying to cover everything the verse alludes to, it will be a better, more readable article. If the verse suggests multiple concepts, save some of them for future articles. In other words, aim to hit the bull's-eye with a rifle rather than a shotgun.

Write about what you know. If you don't know all you would like, do research. Shortly before Columbus Day, I did some reading about Christopher Columbus, his background, his motivations, his relationships, and his various explorations. I came across enough material to provide articles for several Columbus Day emphases over the next few years.

When you write about what you know, your articles are more likely to hold the reader's interest. If the topic doesn't interest you, it certainly won't interest the reader. I have at times been assigned writing projects about passages of Scripture that, at first, did nothing for me personally. However, after study, research, prayer, and meditation, the passage yielded not only interest but also challenge. That's when you can write with conviction because the truth has impacted your own life.

I cannot overstate the importance of discipline in writing devotional articles. By committing myself to write a column every week, I had to do it whether I felt like it or not, whether I felt inspired or not, and whether I had anything to say or not. Some weeks, when no inspiration came, I still typed the title, "Positive Perspective," typed my name under it, double-spaced, and prepared to write the first words. Someone said, "Beginning is half done." It was amazing to me how often that simple discipline triggered some thoughts that eventually gave birth to a full-blown article.

When writers are committed to write regularly, they become more aware of circumstances around them, they are more likely to spawn ideas, and they are more apt to accumulate a bag full of seed thoughts that will sprout and grow into full-blown articles.

Finally, be sure your devotional article reveals something of yourself. A more experienced writer once evaluated my articles by saying, "I see a lot of quotations of other people, but I'm not sure how you feel about the topic. What do you think? Let us know some of your thoughts."

Early in the career of comedian Billy Crystal, he hoped to catch the attention of a well-known agent who represented many famous comedians. When he finally succeeded in meeting with the agent, Billy was expecting to hear compliments for his funny routines. Instead, the agent talked about what they lacked. Crystal was good at impersonating other people, but the agent said his performance lacked anything original that would give audiences any notion of what the comedian himself was thinking and feeling.

When it comes to writing, especially devotionals, it's really not about us. Our aim is to point people to God and His Word. Yet having a personal perspective gives authenticity to our work. It sets us apart from other writers and makes our expressions unique.

Don't be afraid to seek a wider audience for your devotionals. Imagine the beneficial effect if Christians in every community began writing for their local newspapers and other outlets, composing articles that lift the spirit and thoughtfully point people to God and His Word.

A SAMPLE DEVOTIONAL

— Ron McClung —

One of the interesting things about international travel is the opportunity to use a foreign currency. In a restaurant in the United Kingdom, a meal might look appetizing and reasonably priced at seven pounds. However, you must nearly double that price to ascertain the amount in U.S. dollars. When I was in the U.K. last month, the exchange rate was about 1.88 dollars per pound. In other words, for every pound you spend, it costs $1.88 in American money.

On the other hand, the rupee, the basic monetary unit in Pakistan, is quite cheap. It took about 59 rupees to make a dollar last month. If a bricklayer makes 350 rupees a day, it sounds impressive until you realize that is less than six dollars.

The exchange rate not only varies officially from day to day, but if you have your money changed at an exchange bureau, there are also fees to consider. In Great Britain, money changed hands at the rate of two American dollars per pound at an exchange bureau—plus a fee. Not a very good deal.

Some things are worth more than money. An ancient writer believed that God's law was worth more than gold. He used various words for it—law, statutes, ordinances, precepts, commands. They all mean basically the same thing. To our ears, however, it sounds strange that someone would place such value on words. He said, "The ordinances of the LORD are sure and altogether righteous. They are more precious than gold, than much pure gold" (Psalm 19:9–10).

How could words and laws be worth all that? Consider this: if you were speeding down the highway, blissfully unaware that the bridge ahead had been washed out by a storm, and someone had taken the time to put up a sign warning drivers that a bridge was out, how much would that be worth to you? Or, if someone showed you the way to heaven, and it prevented you from taking the downward path to destruction, how much would that be worth? Surely it is worth more than gold, even pure gold!

And the exchange rate? He promises to give me forgiveness in exchange for my sins. You can't beat a deal like that!

10

WRITING COLUMNS AND EDITORIALS

Keith Drury

*Don't be boring. I just wish every journalist who ever wrote anything
started with the assumption that he wasn't gonna keep people all the
way through that unless he really worked hard to keep their interest.*

—Dave Barry

Ice skaters skate, and writers write. Ice skaters improve their craft by skating
—practicing daily to get tiny improvement in style and execution. Writers get
better the same way—by making tiny improvements with regular practice. Of
course everyone who writes does not get better. Some people simply create
more mediocrity. But no writer gets better without writing. One discipline that
improves a writer's writing is a weekly column or editorial. If we commit to
produce a column every week, we'll not be sitting around waiting for inspiration
—we'll get up and go out on the ice and start skating. A weekly column helps
a writer practice their craft. Why not start one this week?

FIND A MARKET

You might aim to eventually become a syndicated columnist for a
Christian magazine or daily newspaper chain, but consider starting simpler
than that—just publish your columns on the Internet. The easiest way to publish
your weekly column is through one of the popular free web log ("blog") sites

like www.blogger.com. When you get rolling and develop an audience, then you can move to something a bit fancier like buying a domain name and getting hosting services for your own site. But start with a free blog site. Writers write. Put it out there and see who wants to read it.

TEST MARKETABILITY

Most writers are like children with crayon drawings. We imagine our work as a masterpiece that ought to be displayed on the world's refrigerator. The truth is most of our writing is mediocre; plenty is downright horrible, and only occasionally is any brilliant. (I've contributed to all three categories but mostly the first two.) It is probably safe to assume your own writing is average and there is probably not much demand for it. Budding writers imagine themselves hitting the jackpot with their brilliant book, but in reality their chances are not much better than winning the lottery. Writing a column allows a writer to gain an audience for whom they can test their writing and find out if anyone really wants to read it. You can discover if your writing is valued by an audience or if it is something only your mother admires. An Internet column allows you to test your marketability. Does anyone want to read what you're writing? Post it and see.

DECIDE THE NATURE OF YOUR COLUMN

What is your angle? What sets your writing apart from the millions of other writers in the world. Decide your approach up front. The invention of the computer has made everybody a writer, and the Internet has made them all publishers. People discharge words into cyberspace at a billion-per-minute rate. What is your angle that will make your words stand out and gather a following?

When I first launched into a weekly Internet column, I decided I'd write columns to provoke people to think—columns that readers might print off and take to lunch to discuss with others. While I sometimes try to convince people, usually I try to prod them to decide what they think about the issue I've addressed. This was not a niche I had found on the Internet; there were no niches in 1995 when I started my column. There were less than a half-dozen religious columns out there at the time. Causing people to think was my aim, so I decided to provoke readers to think more (sometimes I just provoked them).

What would your niche be? What sort of column could you produce every week for years on end? Before you try to get syndicated, see if you have the writer's stamina to produce something every week for a couple of years. Some writers have dazzling ideas, but they only have ten of them. A column forces us to write by discipline, not by inspiration. Pick your niche, and then start writing.

WRITE!

Once you've established the parameters, start writing and never miss. If you're a writer you already know that writing comes by perspiration, not inspiration. Schedule a block of time to write your column, and then post it. I usually allocate two hours to write my weekly column—no more. Sure, when I am writing a manuscript for a book, I take days to polish and craft the words. But for a weekly column, I "just do it," and when two hours is up, I post it.

Perfectionists seldom get published, but writers do.

REVERSE PILATE'S OBSERVATION

One of the wonderful advantages of Internet writing is reversing Pilate's observation, "What is written is written." When an error slips through on paper, we writers must live with it through several reprints and only see it repaired when a second edition is produced. Most books never see a second edition. Internet publishing is more temporary and revisable. Fixing an error is as simple as revising the column and posting it again. Readers sometimes find errors of fact or logic in my columns, and I make corrections within an hour of my first post. I have at times posted ten editions of a column in the first ten days of its life. The Internet is forgiving, which may make it easier to be sloppy, but it also makes it easier to improve.

GET FEEDBACK

If you publish your column on the Internet and people read it, you'll get responses. Generally you will get twenty to thirty "hits" for every person who posts a response or writes an e-mail to you. If you have your own domain and web hosting service, you can actually track the daily traffic on your site.

Because I post my column every Tuesday, my site is overrun with "hits" on that particular day of the week. If you are not up to answering mail, consider omitting your e-mail address and forcing readers to post online. However, using online-only responses means you'll have fewer responses. Readers are more willing to send an e-mail than post a public response.

In 1995 when I began my column I received three or four e-mails a week. Within a year, I was getting fifty e-mails a week. I now get more than one hundred e-mails *a day* from my columns. About half of the responses are to the current week's column, and the other half are to past columns that readers have been steered to by search engines.

One of the interesting responses I get about every month comes from a column I wrote titled, "What to Do When You've Married a Jerk." I've always wondered what people actually type into their search engines that bring them to my column!

If you write something people want to read, they'll respond. And it will hone and sharpen your logic and correct errors in your work. I am a much better writer today than I was ten years ago. Much of that improvement came from readers who took time to correct, scold, chastise, suggest, or rebuke me. I'd rather have them do it than my editor!

PROMOTING YOUR WRITING

Keith Drury

To promote your online column, start by sending an e-mail to your friends, inviting them to read your writing. (If you can't get your friends and relatives to read what you've written, you may not really be a writer after all). Some writers ask other bloggers to add a link to their site to steer more traffic their way. After taking these steps, don't worry too much about promotion. If you write well every week, people will find it. If they like it, they will return. And if you are writing every week, sooner or later you'll produce something that will spread across the Internet at the speed of light.

Some ListServ will pick up your column and send it out, and you'll get a whole new flock of readers. Or Fox News or other online media sites will reference your work, and you'll get inundated with mail and add hundreds of new regular readers. Or you'll write something so controversial that it gets copied and pasted into thousands of e-mails in one day and forwarded to people all around the world, causing your e-mail inbox to collapse. All of these scenarios have actually happened to me.

ANNOUNCE A SELF-IMPOSED DEADLINE

When will you post your column? Pick a day and time when you'll post your column every week, and treat the deadline seriously. I started out in 1995 with "Tuesday Column" as my title, mostly to force me to get something up there every week by Tuesday. My title announced my deadline. I still own the www.TuesdayColumn.com domain name, and many of my long-term readers still enter through that "door," even though I actually use another domain now (DruryWriting.com).

For more than a decade, I've written a column every week (except in the summers when I go backpacking) because I've announced one every Tuesday. I've done some horrible columns and plenty of mediocre ones, but I've also done a few brilliant columns that have had an impact. Set a deadline and stick to it; treat your readers like you would a publisher.

If you just keep writing, sooner or later you'll have an audience. And, after all, there is no such thing as a writer who has no readers.

DON'T WRITE FOR MONEY

Oh, you wanted to make money by writing? Sorry—this is the wrong chapter. But if you follow all of this advice, you could get good enough that some publisher will put some of your writing into a book, or you could get syndicated as a newspaper columnists, which pays about the same rate per hour as a fast food restaurant. Yes, there can be big money in writing for some people. But most writers don't write for the money; they write because they are writers.

11

WRITING MAGAZINE ARTICLES

Andy Scheer

*The only end of writing is to enable readers better to
enjoy life or better to endure it.*

—Samuel Johnson

What's it like to be a magazine editor looking for articles for upcoming issues? It's a lot like checking your e-mail. If you look long enough, you'll eventually find messages you want. But many should never have come to you—and some should never have been sent at all.

For twelve years as managing editor of a large Christian magazine, I had to make sure each issue, cover to cover, was filled with articles our editorial team believed would satisfy our readers. This meant much more, however, than simply finding articles that were biblically sound. Or even biblically sound and well written.

As essential as it is for an article to be biblically sound and well written, the target for our magazine—or any Christian magazine—is much more specific. That's why, unless you're extraordinarily talented—or extraordinarily lucky—you won't find your byline in a magazine you've not taken the time to study. The general interest Christian magazine is gone; in its place are dozens upon dozens of niche publications, each seeking to provide a specific kind of message for a specific group of readers. If "one size fits all" ever applied to Christian magazine writing, it doesn't anymore.

Take teenagers. (I have two.) Each month they receive their own copy of a magazine (from the same publisher) aimed at Christian teens. But while both magazines contain well-written, biblically sound articles, the articles in Karl's magazine seldom resemble the ones in Erica's. While it's obvious that readers of a teen boys' magazine will have different interests than readers of a teen girls' magazine, once the distinction gets much finer than that, many would-be writers miss the mark.

YOUR BEST TARGET MARKETS

But how do writers find that information? Ideally, from the editor's perspective, they're subscribers—or at least regular readers. This means they're not only familiar with the magazine's content and style, they're also part of the target audience. It's easy for their writing to anticipate and meet the readers' needs because those are their needs too.

Say you're a mom with toddlers, and you regularly read a magazine for moms whose children aren't yet in school. One of your recent concerns has been another young mom who has started attending a mothers' support group at your church—even though she comes from a Muslim background and had never before stepped inside a church.

As a writer, you know that what you and your group learned from this experience would interest and benefit the readers of that magazine. And as a regular reader, it's easy for you to discern such aspects for your article as an appropriate length; the most effective voice—first-person narrative, third-person journalistic, or a didactic how-to approach; and whether to cite specific Scriptures to support each of your main points. Unless the magazine's editor has recently said yes to a similar piece, she's likely to welcome such an on-target article.

OTHER MARKETS

Suppose you want to expose the article to a wider audience. Can you simply take a piece written to moms of preschoolers and market it to other magazines? Certainly, but expect mixed results. When I sat in the editor's chair,

I evaluated some 30 proposals each week. We printed only six issues per year, so every two months that added up to 240 articles competing for just seven or eight slots. If an article didn't quite target our readers, it quickly joined the ranks of the 232 unsuccessful applicants.

Our research told us sixty percent of our readers were women and that most were between age 35 and 55. So an article for young moms would miss on two counts. It would not speak to our male readers. And more important, it would fail to relate directly to the majority of our female readers, as most were older. An editor who wants to retain his readers can't afford to print many pieces he knows will appeal to only a few.

Fortunately, writers don't have to take a shot in the dark about whether their article has any hope of fitting what editors seek. Most publications offer *writers guidelines,* usually a multi-page document that specifies their wishes on all the factors we've mentioned, as well as many others. Send a self-addressed, stamped envelope (SASE) and request the guidelines—or check if they're posted on the magazine's website.

But how do you know which magazines are worth your while to investigate in depth? For the Christian market, the indispensable guide is the annual *Christian Writer's Market Guide.* Within its six hundred pages you'll find, not only alphabetical listings of publications, but also listings by magazine categories and topical listings, so you can quickly find which may be interested in articles on Islam, evangelism, moms, or cross-cultural topics.

AHEAD OF THE PACK

This kind of research dramatically increases your likelihood of connecting the right article with the right publication. In my years of screening query letters, I said yes to only about fifteen percent. If the writers had only read our guidelines, the great majority of those queries would have never been sent. Most proposed a topic we didn't cover or a treatment we didn't seek. Or they aimed for a different audience, or suggested a length much too short to cover the topic (or occasionally long enough for a book chapter).

No matter how powerful your profile of an early church leader or how insightful your treatise explaining a Greek word in one of Paul's letters, it rates an automatic rejection from a magazine that prints only first-person accounts. Ditto on essays, exhortations, Bible studies, and biographies. If the magazine is written specifically for laity, don't propose articles that apply only to pastors, or overseas missionaries, or children's Sunday school teachers. Obvious advice? Not for most prospective freelance writers.

NOT ONLY WHAT IT'S ABOUT . . .

The question I most often heard from writers was, "Are you interested in an article about . . .?" Editors, however, need to know not only what an article is *about;* they need to know what it's *for*. You may see other labels, such as *takeaway* or *application*, but I think it's easiest to think in terms of *purpose*. What do you want the article to accomplish in the life of your reader?

If you can't define that in a single sentence, perhaps it's because your article lacks a clear purpose. Or maybe it tries to accomplish too much. With its relatively short length, a magazine article needs a tight, single focus. As you describe your article, if you find yourself mentioning several topics, several audiences, or several purposes, you have a problem. Go back, pick a single, main purpose, then make sure everything in your article advances that goal.

Having trouble fitting your article into the required length? Make sure each sentence, each paragraph, and each section advances your stated purpose. Anything that doesn't, doesn't belong. Near the end of his Gospel, the apostle John speaks of omitting interesting material about Jesus—because it wasn't key to fulfilling his purpose.

> Jesus did many other things as well. If every one of them were written down, I suppose that even the whole world would not have room for the books that would be written" (John 21:25).

> Jesus did many other miraculous signs in the presence of his disciples, which are not recorded in this book. But these are written that you may believe that Jesus is the Christ, the Son of God, and that by believing you may have life in his name" (John 20:30–31).

CAPTURING AND KEEPING INTEREST

Even if your article passes all these tests, it faces a final challenge: It has to be interesting. Remember the last time you glanced at an article, and then flipped the page? And remember that other article you couldn't stop reading? Afterward you made copies and told friends about it. That's the kind of writing editors seek.

An article has perhaps ten second to grab a reader's attention. Editors want articles that grab readers—and keep them grabbed. Great topics aren't enough. Ask yourself, "Would I want to read my article if someone else had written it?" You know your mom, your spouse, or your best friend would read it. Editors want articles everyone else wants to read too.

Editors want writing that breathes life into a topic—not rehashes material they've read before. Proposing an article about Christmas? Make it different than the "Let's Put Christ Back in Christmas" article that you, the editor, and the magazine's readers have seen dozens of times. The same goes for other important, but perennial topics, such as supporting missionaries, opposing abortion, or strengthening marriages. Take a fresh approach. Make the lead paragraph something unexpected.

A few years back, *Focus on the Family* printed "When Feathers Fly" by Janet E. Pratt, examining principles for couples to resolve their conflicts. The topic and points of application were pretty standard. What hooked readers was Pratt's anecdotal lead, in which she described needing to cooperate with her husband (to whom she wasn't speaking) to haul off the carcass of a dead ostrich. (Maybe a ho-hum lead for *Today's Ostrich Rancher,* but for *Focus,* it was arresting.)

Some 650 words later, as Pratt concluded her anecdote, readers stuck with her as she turned the corner: "Immediately afterward, as I showered off the dead bird smell, it occurred to me that the principles of handling conflicts in a marriage are a lot like the mechanics of dealing with a dead ostrich."

Your experience may not include anything like a dead ostrich. (Count yourself blessed.) But if your topic is worth reading about, you can still find a fresh way to approach it. Maybe there's a dramatic quote from a neighbor or an expert on the topic. Maybe it's a brief story about an argument with a co-worker that prompted you to see a passage of Scripture in a fresh way.

Then once you've hooked a reader, maintain interest with the standard elements of good writing: concrete nouns, vivid verbs, sentence variety, specific examples, and consistent, logical development. You don't need gimmicks. Christian editors (and readers) look for accounts that find a topic's human dimension, apply God's living Word, then convey that information in simple, powerful, straightforward language.

Earn a reputation for that kind of writing, and editors will welcome your next article.

NARRATIVES WITH APPLICATION

 Andy Scheer

One easy way to give an article an interesting, human dimension is to use storytelling. Rather than a third-person, directive, how-to article such as "How to Evangelize Your Neighbor," consider a first-person, "How I Reached My Neighbor" narrative.

FINDING TOPICS

How can you find topics for an application-driven narrative? Here are some key questions to ask yourself. The answers should help point you to potential topics for application-driven narratives—and the elements to emphasize.

WHAT DID YOU LEARN?

Look for areas where you can see a significant difference from where you were "then" to where you are now? (These may be internal, regarding your thought life, or concerning family, friends, co-workers, or neighbors.) How did you come to that realization? What was it like putting it into practice?

WHAT DIFFICULTIES DID YOU ENCOUNTER?

Avoid pat answers. Beware of a self-congratulatory tone. But also avoid self-deprecation.

WHAT WAS THE EFFECT ON YOU AND THOSE AROUND YOU?

"Before" scenes could serve as opening anecdotes to hook readers. "After" scenes provide specific incentives for others to apply what you've learned.

WHAT CAN OTHERS LEARN THROUGH MY EXPERIENCE?

Include the key, scriptural principles others can apply in their own situations.

12

WRITING PERSONAL EXPERIENCE STORIES

Hal Hostetler

Writers end up writing about their obsessions. Things that haunt them; things they can't forget; stories they carry in their bodies waiting to be released.

—Natalie Goldberg

How many times have you heard someone say, "That's a wonderful testimony. You *must* write it up. I'm sure [insert name of magazine here] will publish it in a minute." Or get this: A beginning writer sends a manuscript to an editor saying, "God told me to send this to you. Please publish it in your next edition."

Well, as an editor, I've heard many such comments, and believe me, writing for publication isn't that simple. The writer may very well have a story worth telling, and if written in the proper style, it could get published. But to write a good personal-experience story, every writer needs to know and understand the basics of good storytelling.

My purpose here is to give you those basics.

DO YOU HAVE A STORY TO TELL?

Before you even begin to write your story, decide where you want to submit the manuscript. It's a good idea to get a copy or two of the target publications and study the style of their stories. What types of stories do they publish? Action/drama? Business? Medical/healing? Sports? Stories about relationships or learning experiences, or overcoming some difficulty or handicap? Match the category of your story to the magazine that seems most likely to publish it.

Next, determine not to write a simple testimony. A story is different from a testimony. Giving an oral testimony is often a recollection of what happened, usually in the order in which it happened. Writing a story, however, requires preparation and planning. Ask yourself a few questions: "Do I really have a story to tell? What's its point? Who will want to read it? How will it help the reader?"

If the answer to the first question is yes, you've taken the first step. But then you need to know how to write it. A good way to begin is to try to think like a fiction writer. Even though you're not writing fiction, the techniques of fiction form the foundation of a good story. That requires more than *telling* what happened; it means *showing* the reader exactly what happened. It should be written from a single point of view, beginning with a question or problem of interest to the reader, developing a plot, portraying the main character in the story in a way the reader can sympathize with, using description and dialogue, creating you-are-there scenes, and building suspense as the story moves toward a climax that illustrates an important point.

You will also need to consider the following ingredients of a good story: theme, plot, conflict, characters, scenes, description, dialog, suspense, climax, a definite conclusion, and a "takeaway."

WHAT'S YOUR TAKEAWAY?

Why do I emphasize "takeaway"? For good reason. Christian editors today are looking for stories that contain a takeaway—a message that readers can take away from the story and apply to their own life. This means you, as the writer, need to determine ahead of time if your story contains such a message. Try to visualize your reader and ask yourself how your story will help that person. Perhaps what you've experienced will provide a lesson in gaining spiritual insight, relating to God better, dealing with various kinds of trouble, or learning how to overcome problems such as fear, worry, impatience, or other negative feelings you've conquered in your own life with God's help.

Or, if you are ghostwriting a story for someone else, you'll probably have to identify the takeaway yourself before writing the story of the person you've interviewed.

Recall the parables of Jesus in the Gospels. The parable of the Good Samaritan, for instance, has a very explicit takeaway. Loving our neighbors includes showing compassion on those who are unlike us, who may be from a group we don't associate with. The parable of the prodigal son demonstrates how showing mercy and forgiveness (the father) offers restoration to a person who has sinned against us (the prodigal son) and reassurance to those who exhibit bad behavior such as jealousy (the older brother). So plan to tell your story as Jesus did—leaving a helpful point in the reader's mind.

PLANNING YOUR MANUSCRIPT

In the planning process, determine the takeaway first. In fact, it's a good idea to write it at the very beginning of your manuscript and put a box around it, if your word processing software has such a function. Then, as you write, occasionally scroll back up to the takeaway box to make sure your story is on track. That box is there to keep you focused, to prevent you from going off on a tangent. The final takeaway of the story doesn't have to read exactly like the one you've written ahead of time; it should blend in with the rest of the story, but it may even be implied rather than stated specifically. After the story is complete and you're satisfied with the manuscript, delete the takeaway box.

Next, it's time to do some plotting. What is the thrust of your story? Is it to reach a goal? If so, what's standing in the way? Develop a number of scenes showing what obstacles you had to overcome in reaching the goal. Alternatively, the plot might involve the need to be delivered from some kind of trouble. In either of these cases, show how God came to your aid when things looked the bleakest. The scenes should show the obstacles becoming more and more difficult until, at the climax, something happens to change things—and the main character—for the better.

Please note: All plots involve conflict. It may be between you and another person, or a physical limitation, an illness, a natural disaster such as a flood or tornado, or the aftermath of an accident. It may even involve inner conflicts such as fear, doubt, or insecurity.

A story requires characters. Who is the main character in your story? If the story is about your own experience, then you are the main character. Who are the other important characters, such as those who have a role in the story's outcome? Give them names, even if only first names. In a short story, readers tend to lose track of characters if there are more than two or three. All other characters, therefore, will only have labels, such as "the policeman" or "my uncle." These characters may appear briefly in the story, but they have only minor roles, and their actions do not figure in the outcome. Flesh out the named characters so the reader can identify with them, especially the main character.

PUTTING IT INTO WORDS

When you begin to write, don't worry about the title. Entitle it whatever you want, but do so to identify the story, not to impress the editor. If the magazine buys your manuscript, the editors will write their own title in keeping with the flow of articles or stories in that particular issue.

What *is* all-important, however, is the first page.

In the beginning of your story, gaining the editor's attention is your primary goal. If you can't captivate the editor on that page with the promise of an interesting and perhaps exciting story, you've lost your first battle. The opening may even suggest to the reader that what you are about to reveal is something that will change his or her life. It should also introduce conflict and gain the reader's sympathy for the main character. And write it in a language everyone can understand, without using religious jargon. Too much "church talk" can drive away the very reader you're trying to reach.

From here on, think in terms of scenes. Narrative can speed the story along, but it doesn't give the reader the full picture. Scenes allow you to invite the reader into your story, to experience what you experienced, to see and hear, perhaps even smell, the world in which your story took place. In writing a scene, add description, dialogue, and action to bring the story to life and to move it along.

A word about dialogue: Use it sparingly. If the magazine you plan to submit the story to has a 1,500-word limit, you don't have enough space to carry on a drawn-out conversation. Only use dialogue that keeps the story moving.

BUILDING TOWARD A CLIMAX

Try to build suspense that will keep the reader guessing how the story might end. At the end of each scene the reader should be wondering what comes next. Each scene should build toward a dramatic climax where something happens to change everything and bring about the solution to the problem that was introduced in the opening paragraphs. But that change should not be an internal coming-to-realize event. Whatever changes the situation must come from outside. A friend gives a good piece of advice or God impresses on you a verse of Scripture you had never noticed before. If the story requires someone to come to your rescue, how was God involved in sending that person?

This is where the story ends. In winding it up, make sure the takeaway is clear. If it isn't evident in what you've already written, you might add a brief closing scene that demonstrates how the experience has affected your life, and how it could change the life of a reader in a similar situation.

That's all there is to it. If you follow these guidelines, you have an excellent chance of seeing your story in print.

Sample Personal Experience Story

Hal Hostetler

"Why?" I kept asking God as I climbed the concrete steps of an unfamiliar church in Midtown Manhattan. "Why won't you heal my daughter?"

Kristal, a teenager, had been suffering for a year and a half from Lyme disease, which caused excruciating headaches, muscle pain, and an inability to concentrate. No amount of prayer seemed to help. Now discouragement had cast a pall over our whole family.

Inside, the sanctuary was alive with activity, not the place of quiet I had anticipated. Dozens of people were walking up and down the center aisle, talking. Sliding into a pew near the back, I tried to ignore the distractions. My eyes focused on the cross at the front, and again I prayed for Kristal's healing. Then I waited in silence.

Events of the past year and a half played in my mind: the red bite on her arm, which we thought was from a spider in our backyard in New Jersey. Her increasing pain, especially headaches that no medication would relieve. And the first night my wife Carol and I awoke to hear her sobbing in her room across the hall. We hurried over. "I can't stand it anymore, Dad," she said through tears. Carol hugged her, then got an ice pack for her. Together we prayed for her healing as I placed my hand on her shoulder.

But she wasn't healed. During the next year she was hospitalized three times. She missed her whole junior year of high school. Carol and I fought with the school board for five months to get a tutor to help her catch up on her studies. All of her friends stopped coming or calling. "I think everybody has forgotten me, including God," she moaned.

Carol and I felt helpless. In her senior year Kristal was hospitalized twice more and missed so many days of school that her guidance counselor feared she wouldn't be able to graduate.

So there I sat in a noisy church pleading with God again for her healing.

And then came the still, small voice I hadn't heard for some time. *Get rid of your resentments and you will be healed,* said the voice in my mind. I recognized it instantly.

That evening at home I explained what I'd heard to Carol, Kristal, and her older sister, Laurel. We all needed healing, and we talked about the resentments we carried in our hearts. The friends who had abandoned Kristal. The school board that almost refused to grant her a tutor because of a technicality: her doctor couldn't write an excuse that would set a date for her return to class. We wrote everything down on slips of paper, prayed, confessed our resentments to God, and forgave those who had hurt us. Then we tossed the papers into the lighted fireplace. As we watched their smoke rising into the chimney, the pall began to lift.

Over the next couple of months Kristal's symptoms gradually went away. She graduated from high school and college, got a job with a large computer firm, and married her college sweetheart. And it all came about as a result of really hearing God and acting on his instructions. Removing the spiritual barrier had allowed him to answer our prayers.

13

WRITING HUMOR

Jerry Brecheisen

Humor is a rubber sword—it allows you to make a point without drawing blood.

—Mary Hirsch

D id you hear the one about the pregnant senior citizen?

You see, humor isn't a new genre. The oldest and best book in history, the Bible, has its sprinklings of humor. After the aged biblical matriarch, Sarah, learned that she got a passing grade on her pregnancy test, she had a talk with Abraham, the aged father, and explained, "God has brought me laughter, and everyone who hears about this will laugh with me" (Gen. 21:6).

And ol' Abe had a belly laugh of his own. Now he'd not only be cashing Social Security checks to pay for throw-away diapers, he'd have to trade his one-humped camel sedan for a treasured two-humped camel SUV.

The Bible's Author is known to laugh. Psalm 2:4 says, "The One enthroned in heaven laughs . . ." God has a sense of humor? You bet! He not only invented the zebra, ostrich, and aardvark as humorous props, He taught his creation how to laugh. He knows the value of humor in soothing the human spirit. He knows that a mix of laughter and life will make the journey to Canaan even more tolerable. He planned for it. He gifted writers like you to minister to time travelers with words that reflect both his character and compassion.

Timing is important in everything. God invented that as well. Ecclesiastes 3:4 says there is "a time to laugh." So humor has its topics and its timing. Christian writers who conquer both can turn a frown upside down for someone who has hit a speed bump in life so hard that it knocked a Starbucks coffee out of the cup holder in the console of their compact car. And they may also join a list of Christian authors who have climbed up the greased pole of best-seller lists.

Thank God for the Barbara Johnsons, who have taught us about "lite" reading, and its positive effect on the soul. She, along with her writing peers, administer the antidote for planetary living prescribed in the Word, "A cheerful heart is good medicine, but a crushed spirit dries up the bones" (Prov. 17:22). So go ahead, fight osteoporosis of the heart with some well-planned humor writing!

Humor is like a pair of pantyhose—I'm told. If it fits, the journey will be pleasant; but if it doesn't fit, it will put you in a bind. Let's talk about fit. Humor writing is a craft, a journey, and a ministry—one that could turn the partly cloudy days into partly sunny. Let's look first to the craft.

UNDERSTAND THE PURPOSE OF HUMOR

Humor isn't an "instead of;" rather, it is an "in addition to." Having the insights of a cross-eyed tsetse fly, I struggle with deep philosophical conversations. When I lunch with well-lettered friends, my contribution is usually a "yep" and a nod. But I've discovered that humor writing can even be an asset to their academic acumen—not to replace their treatises or expositions, but to provide an "in addition to." In other words, I can offer a funny line that may sharpen their reader's attention to a discourse on the long-term health benefits of watching reality TV.

Humor writing is icing on the cake. It contrasts the doughy substances of other writing. It isn't necessarily designed to inspire deep, dark thoughts. It's there to add a cool breeze, to take maudlin minds off the mundane or miserable.

BE AWARE OF THE TRENDS

The humor writer must keep a close eye on what makes people laugh (or what people buy). Humor writers can't watch TV, listen to the radio, or read humorous stories the way others do. We observe the premise. We catalog the set-ups — and the "end-ups." We note words. We watch phrases *turn*. We look at book titles on best-seller lists. We search for the common (and current) threads that run through the diatribes, dialogues, and ditsy writings that strike a popularity chord with people. We have a plan:

WE CLIP

We know that a highlighted phrase — accidental or intentional — in a humorous magazine article or newspaper column makes a good addition to our "idea" file. And we know that it will come in handy when we need an article title or chapter heading.

WE KEEP

We write down the funny thoughts of others — not to "copy," but to comprehend, and to put a similar thought or situation into our own words. We may organize our notes in a folder (electronic or otherwise), or we may keep them in a notebook over the sun visor. We know that good idea files are gold mines.

WE CATEGORIZE

We used to say, "Now, where did I put that?" Finding that line about male menopause in a file full of quotes was like trying to find the right "John Smith" in a New York telephone directory. Now we organize clips and quotes — in categorized files.

PRACTICE DESCRIBING A PERSON, PLACE, OR THING

Humorous writing focuses on details. It's one thing to write about Miss Crabby sitting down in the pew following the opening prayer at your church. It's another to *paint the picture with words*. For example, "When the Reverend said his familiar "A-a-a-a-men," Miss Crabby seemed to collapse into the pew in layers — like the implosion of an old football stadium."

You may have an antique in your house that is as weird as it is wonderful. Your mother gave it to you as a keepsake, but you've been hoping that your youngest child would knock it over during a tempter tantrum. Practice your writing by describing the ugly pass-along, looking for every funny detail.

KEEP THE AUDIENCE IN MIND

Writings about the bunions, bulges, and bifocals of middle-age aren't necessarily for every age group. The young adult set may be more interested in biceps, beauty marks, and beef substitutes. Determining your audience is important. Who are they? Young? Old? Educated? Underachieved? Married? Single? Write to *them*.

- Start with the familiar.
- Use current-event topics.
- Write about common experiences.
- Make sure the reader identifies with your words and phrases.

KEEP IT SIMPLE

You may have some funny branches at the top of your family tree, but don't wear the reader out in making the climb. Fewer words are often better than more words. Smaller sentences are easier to read than the larger. You might even use a single-word paragraph—with an appropriate punctuation mark—to say it with flair.

Really!

For example, *"Monkey feathers!"* isn't a phrase we use at the water cooler. But it could be used in the description of a first meeting with a pompous person. A two-word paragraph may emphasize that person's need of an attitude adjustment on the level of an extreme makeover.

AMPLIFY THE ABSURD

Humor writing isn't just about describing the *everyday* and *everyone*. It's about putting a firecracker under both, *unexpectedly* lighting the fuse, and watching the show! Stretch the expression. A long nose becomes "a nose longer than a fire hose." Drinking a cup of coffee turns into "fueling up for a caffeinated hissy-fit."

Use caution, however, not to describe people with slurs of any kind. You are a *Christian* writer. You pay your respects to all of God's creation. You can even portray the biblical account of Eutychus falling asleep while listening to the longest sermon in the Apostle Paul's career (Acts 20:7–12), without referring to his "Hooked on Phonics" degree.

You also need to preserve anonymity. You may have a whole household—or an office-full—of subjects worthy of a gigantic jab in a sentence or paragraph, but they should remain anonymous, even to the point of altering the DNA of their physical or psychological characteristics.

Author and comedian, Steven Wright, said, "There's a fine line between fishing and just standing on the shore like an idiot." You're not standing on the shore. You're fishing. You're a writer. You have a God-given interest, and the practiced ability, to *fish*—to pull back the curtains of uncertain times and let some *Son* shine in. And you can do it in such a way that it not only exercises some facial muscles, but also affects a heart. Be as funny as you can, as long as you bring your readers back to the wonderful and consuming hope of the gospel. The "Word became flesh," with enough grace, glory, and applied humor to let people like you and me see a holy, just, and merciful God, who sympathizes with our human situations, and solves earthly problems with eternal solutions.

We are a people who will finish the race with a smile—maybe laughter. Isaiah 35:10 says, "And the ransomed of the LORD will return. They will enter Zion with singing; everlasting joy will crown their heads. Gladness and joy will overtake them, and sorrow and sighing will flee away."

And as they say in the funnies, "That's all, folks!"

WRITING THE GAG

Jerry Brecheisen

Humor writing is usually a composite of gags: humorous incidents based on people or events, real or imagined. They may run from a few sentences, to a paragraph, to an entire chapter. If you look carefully at a cartoon, you'll notice the ingredients of the gag: the characters, the setting, the storyline or dialogue, and the pay-off. The same principle applies to humor writing. Every writer has his or her game plan for putting gags into an article or book. Here's one:

DETERMINE THE AUDIENCE

Who will identify with this gag or story? How will it relate to the audience's life experience? Will they be able to see themselves in this situation? Will it offend anyone?

START WITH THE CHARACTERS

What is there about the characters that will add to the gag/story? How can they be described in such a way that the reader will not only identify with the characters, but will also laugh at their fortunes or foibles?

ENVISION THE SETTING

Ask, "How can I turn a typical setting into a (riotously) funny incident? How can I describe the place in an untypical way? What word "props" can I add? How will the characters move about the place?

ADD THE DIALOGUE

Decide whether the script will be in the first, second, or third person. What part of the country will the characters come from? How will the characters interact? How can I add "tension" to the dialogue of the characters? How will I describe their attitudes?

THINK ABOUT THE "PAY-OFF"

Where is the gag/story heading? How will it end? How will that ending hit the funny bone of the reader?

APPEAL TO THE SENSES

What sights, sounds, or smells could I add that the reader will immediately identify with? How can I put my reader "on site" mentally and emotionally?

THINK ABOUT THE SURPRISE ENDING

Similar to a comical pratfall, the writer of a gag/story will include a "sudden turn of events." An unexpected action or reaction is at the core of good humor writing.

For each writer, the writing journey will have its own path. Some will start with a road map, while others will venture out like the stereotypical husband who refuses to ask for directions. The humor writer will discover what works for her or him. Whatever the way, the basic direction always starts with an *introduction*, proceeds to a *description or dialogue*, and ends with a *surprise*.

One way to develop your own "gag writing" skill is to watch for gags in a humorous article or book. Notice how the author sets up the plot, how the characters are introduced, how the author describes the characters, and how the author leads the reader to the "pay-off" and the "surprise ending."

PRACTICE MAKES FUNNY

The second phase of developing humor-writing skill is the hardest: practice. Luckily, the practice won't involve piano scales—with hours in front of a piano teacher whose last laugh was when President Lincoln tripped on the stairway leading to the Ford Theater balcony. Published writers are practicing writers. They write most—if not all—of the time, carefully crafting words, sentences, paragraphs, and pages. Think about it, you can add a humorous punch line to the world of someone who is used to just getting punched. And that's a ministry.

14

WRITING
SCREENPLAYS

James Scott Bell

*Theaters are the new Church of the Masses—where people sit
huddled in the dark listening to people in the light tell
them what it is to be human.*

—1930s theater critic

So you want to write a screenplay. You long to hear a famous director take your timeless pages and yell, "Action!"

Welcome to the world of everybody.

At least that's true where I live. The unofficial definition of "screenwriter" is "anybody in Los Angeles with opposable thumbs."

But though the odds against seeing one of your screenplays make it to the screen remain extremely long (it has always been so), you can increase your chances by making sure your screenplay has a story that will sustain interest for the length required (anywhere from half an hour to two hours or more) and a structure that makes the story accessible to the audience.

So story and structure are the two essentials.

Without a story, it doesn't matter how well structured your script is. We've all seen movies that are dreadful, even though they came from well-structured scripts.

On the other hand, a good story idea can get lost in a maze of poor execution, which is a structural problem.

Let's look at these in more detail.

STORY

It's beyond the scope of this chapter to lay out all the elements of a good story, but let me give you a few guidelines.

ORIGINALITY

Are you rehashing a plot that's been done? Congratulations. That's what Shakespeare did too. All the plots have been done, to one degree or another. But bringing fresh elements to the plot is what will set yours apart. And that's where characters come in.

CHARACTERS THAT COMPEL

Stories are about characters dealing with threat or challenge. The fresher your characters, the more original your story will seem to your readers, even if the plot is familiar to them.

HIGH STAKES

Make sure your lead character has *a lot* to lose. The more important the stakes, the more the audience will care.

SURPRISES

The audience needs to see things they don't anticipate—twists and turns that make them sit up and keep watching.

HEART

If your story lacks a "passionate center" (and this comes from *you)* it will not reach the heights it otherwise could. Do you care about your own story? You should if you're going to write an entire screenplay.

Now, take all of the above, shake, and pour into a structure that will give your story the best chance to connect with an audience.

STRUCTURE

You can't go wrong with the traditional three-act structure. It has stood the test of time, ever since Aristotle (who never sold a screenplay) mapped out the drama.

In modern screenplays, Act 1 usually takes up one quarter of the entire running time (the first thirty minutes of a two-hour movie). Act 2 is fully one half. The last act runs the other quarter.

Briefly, here is what each act should be about. I'll use the academic terms *beginning, middle,* and *end.*

BEGINNINGS

Beginnings get us connected to the lead. Think of memorable movie openings. Usually, you have interesting characters involved in some sort of challenging situation. In other words, it's not merely normal life, but something *more.*

This can be called the opening "disturbance." Cinematic life, without disturbance, is dull.

At the beginning of *The Wizard of Oz,* we see Dorothy running home to her farm with her dog, Toto. Why? Because the awful Miss Gulch has threatened to get rid of the dog. When Miss Gulch actually arrives to take Toto away, that's the disturbance to Dorothy's world. We have an instant affinity with her because of this threat. We begin to care about the lead character.

Beginnings have other tasks to perform. The four most important are—

- Present the story world. (Tell us something about the setting, the time, and the immediate context.)
- Establish the movie's tone. (Is this to be a sweeping epic or a zany farce? Action packed or character driven?)
- Hook the viewers so they are compelled to keep watching.
- Introduce the opposition. (Who or what wants to stop the lead?)

MIDDLES

The major part of the movie is the confrontation, a series of battles between the lead and the opposition. This happens in Act 2.

Some wise scribe once said that a plot has a beginning, a *muddle,* and an end—a good phrase to keep in mind. You want trouble in the middle, lots of it. Trouble is what makes the audience worry about the lead character. And if the audience is worried, you've got them hooked.

The middle is also where subplots bloom, adding complexity to the film and usually reflecting the deeper meaning of the whole.

Throughout the middle, the plot strands weave in and out of the narrative, creating a feeling of inevitability, while at the same time surprising the audience in various ways. In addition, the middle should—

- Deepen character relationships
- Keep us caring about what happens
- Set up the final battle that will wrap things up at the end.

ADHESIVE

If the lead character can solve the problem simply by resigning from the action, the audience will wonder why he or she doesn't do so. Or, if there is not a strong enough reason for the lead character to continue, the viewer won't be all that worried.

There needs to be a strong reason for the lead character to *stick around*.

I call this crucial structural element *adhesive*, because it keeps all the elements bonded together. You need it to keep the characters together throughout that long muddle.

Another name that has been given to this element is "the crucible," the arena of conflict. If you have carefully selected an objective that is essential to the well-being of the lead, and an opposition with an equally valid reason to stop the lead, your adhesive will usually be self-evident.

But here are a few tips to make that connection strong.

Life and death. If the opposition has a strong enough reason to kill the lead, that's an automatic adhesive. Staying alive is essential to one's well-being.

Professional duty. The audience understands why a lawyer who takes on a client cannot just walk away. The same goes for a cop assigned a case.

Moral duty. If a young girl is kidnapped, for example, we understand why her mother doesn't walk away from the action. She will do whatever it takes to get her child back.

Physical location. In Steven King's *The Shining*, a husband, wife, and child take jobs as caretakers at a mountain hotel that gets snowed in every winter. They physically can't get away from the action. *Casablanca* is another such story. No one can get out of Casablanca without permission or "Letters of Transit."

As an example of the crucial nature of adhesive, consider the film of Neil Simon's play *The Odd Couple*. Oscar Madison is a happy slob. He lives in a bachelor pad where he and his friends can be as sloppy as they want. They can smoke cigars, play cards, and make a mess.

Felix Unger, Oscar's friend, is a neat freak. When he moves into Oscar's apartment, sparks fly. The two do not get along. This is the engine of the conflict.

The obvious question is, why doesn't Oscar just kick Felix out? It's Oscar's apartment, after all. If he can't stand Felix, why not show him the door?

Simon, recognizing the need for adhesive, cleverly sets it up from the start. Felix's wife has left him, and he is suicidal. Oscar and the others are worried about Felix being left alone.

Thus, Oscar, Felix's friend, undertakes an understandable moral task— watching out for Felix.

Of course, the humor of the play occurs as Oscar reaches the point where he feels like killing Felix himself.

In character-driven films, the adhesive will sometimes be self-generating. A lead must change on the inside or suffer psychological loss. Or she must get away from an influence (the opposition) that threatens to squelch her growth. This is the conflict in the classic Warner Bros. film *Now, Voyager* starring Bette Davis. Davis must overcome the influence of a domineering mother in order to become her own person.

Some other examples include *Jaws*, in which Sheriff Brody has a professional duty to protect the residents and tourists of his town from the shark that terrorizes the beaches. And in *The Fugitive,* the adhesive is the law. Richard Kimble (Harrison Ford) is innocent of his wife's murder. It's not only self-interest that keeps him on the run; he also has a moral duty to find the man who killed his wife. On the other side, Sam Gerard (Tommy Lee Jones) is a U.S. Marshal, and thus has a professional duty to catch the fugitive. We well understand why neither character can just walk away.

ENDS

The last act of the movie gives us the resolution of the big story.

The best endings tie up all loose ends. Are there story threads that are left dangling? You must either resolve these in a way that does not distract from the main plot line, or go back and snip them out. Readers have long memories.

As well as tying up loose ends, the best endings also give a feeling of resonance. What does the story *mean* in the larger sense?

And there you have it. Simple, yes?

In concept, it is. There is a natural flow to the three-act structure. You know more about it than you think due to all the movies you've seen and the novels you've read.

The hard part is putting your own stamp on the story, your personal voice and vision, along with fresh twists and dynamic characters.

But put all that in a screenplay and who knows? Someday you may hear that director, the one holding your script, yell, "Action!"

EDITOR'S NOTE: Several good books detail the exact format a movie script must take as well as how to market a screenplay.

THE WIZARDRY OF OZ

—————— James Scott Bell ——————

Here is how the structural elements line up in the classic movie *The Wizard of Oz*.

ACT I

OPENING SCENE

We meet Dorothy, a girl who lives on a farm in Kansas with her aunt and uncle, a dog named Toto, and some goofy farmhands. She dreams of someday going to a place "over the rainbow."

DISTURBANCE

Miss Gulch arrives by bicycle, demanding that Toto be turned over to her so she can have him "destroyed." Her demand is backed up by the law, so Uncle Henry reluctantly gives Toto to Miss Gulch. Dorothy is devastated.

But Toto escapes from Miss Gulch's basket and runs back to the farm. Dorothy, knowing it could happen again, decides to run away. She meets the Professor, who engineers a little "magic" to induce Dorothy to return home.

She and Toto get back just as the big twister hits. Dorothy gets knocked in the head, and thus enters through the first doorway of no return. The twister picks up the house and lands her and Toto in a Technicolor world called Oz.

ACT II

THE "MUDDLE"

The "muddle" of *The Wizard of Oz* is all about Dorothy trying to get to the wizard so she can find a way home. Along the way she encounters plenty of trouble. There's a wicked witch who wants to stop her, some apple throwing trees, a lion with more bark than bite, and so on. She picks up some allies along the way, including a scarecrow, a tin man, the aforementioned lion, and a good witch. The trouble increases when Dorothy and her friends finally get to see the wizard and he delivers some bad news. Before he'll help her, she and her allies have to bring him the broomstick of the Wicked Witch of the West.

So they set out through a dark forest, and then they fall through the second doorway of no return; Dorothy is captured by flying monkeys and taken away.

ACT III

The final battle has been set up. The three allies—the scarecrow, tin man, and lion—must find a way to save Dorothy from the witch. They get inside the castle, where things go wrong again, and it looks like they're all going to die at the hands of the witch and her minions. But then the witch goes too far, setting the scarecrow aflame. Dorothy throws water on him, but also douses the witch. And we all know what happens then!

This is not quite the end. There's a little twist that gives an added measure of suspense. The wizard is not a wizard at all! He's just that "man behind the curtain"—a fraud! But he says he'll take Dorothy home personally.

Then another twist! The balloon that's supposed to carry them both is unloosed, and only the "wizard" is carried away. Dorothy seems stranded in Oz.

But then the good witch shows up again and tells her about the heel clicking thing. Whew. Dorothy finally gets home, and says that's where she's going to stay.

15

WRITING A NONFICTION BOOK

Sharon Norris Elliott

There ain't nothing more to write about, and I am rotten glad of it, because if I'd a knowed what a trouble it was to make a book I wouldn't a tackled it, and ain't a-going to no more.

—Mark Twain as Huckleberry Finn

M arion Zimmer Bradley got it right when he said, "Writing is like everything else; ten percent inspiration or talent, and ninety percent hard work." Yes, remember this: 10 percent inspiration; 90 percent perspiration. I would love it if all I had to do was let my brilliance and vision tumble out onto the page, hand those pages to my editor, and leave the mundane detail of sorting it all out to her.

To my dismay, I have discovered that is not the case with me. The very fact that you are reading this book is proof that that is not the case with you either. Your brilliant visions are just that—visions—and will remain so if you don't bring those mountain-top experiences down to the valley of writing reality where well-crafted paragraphs, interesting sentence structure, correct spelling, and proper punctuation live. Until you wrap your visions in the reality of language, they will continue to excite you but will never move me because they will never get to me.

We're here to discuss doing that through the medium of the written word in non-fiction book form.

You can spend hours mulling over your opening line and rack your brain trying to turn a clever phrase, or you can expend that necessary perspiration working smarter, not harder. You need a way to corral your thoughts, organize them neatly, and get back to working with them whenever you need to. Storyboarding will do just that.

Storyboarding was popularized by Walt Disney who decided that he needed to see the progress of his animators any time he walked into their studio. He accomplished this, not by peeking over their shoulders, but by having them pin their pictures up on the walls. Disney could pass through the studio and see the story being acted out as it was being created. Any scenes he didn't like, he simply tore off of the wall and replaced them with something else.

The storyboarding idea has remained a staple in the creation of visual entertainment, but has been adopted by many other industries. The adaptation of this organizational tool for writing books revolutionized my writing, as I'm sure it will yours.

THE SENSE

There are two reasons storyboarding makes sense. First, it makes sense to have a concrete plan and an easy-to-follow outline. It is essential for you as the author to have a crystal clear idea of where you want your book to take your reader. Storyboarding allows you to see your own ideas and helps you to stay on track as you write.

Second, it makes sense to allow others to participate in your planning. You may ask, why should I want my ideas out in the open for the entire world to see? The answer is easy. You're writing your book for the entire world to see. You're not writing it for yourself, so why should you keep even the planning to yourself? Others can look at your storyboard, encourage you as you write, and even suggest ideas you may not have considered.

Consider putting together a focus group of people who are members of the audience for which you are writing. Solicit ideas from them to ascertain what they feel they would need from a book on your topic. Gather their ideas in steps two through six detailed below.

THE SETUP

A storyboard is an amazingly flexible, highly visible planning tool, and setting one up in your home is easy. Mount a corkboard or cork squares on an available wall. Purchase three-by-five index cards—white or colored, lined or not—and some push-pins. That's it. Don't panic, though, if you don't have a wall space. Any large, flat surface will do, such as a table or even the floor. If you'd like, you can substitute sticky notes for index cards and just attach the papers right to the wall or a sliding glass door. As we go through the steps, you'll understand what you'll be doing with these supplies.

THE STEPS

STEP ONE: DEFINE TOPIC

It is essential to have a clear idea of what your book is about. Be able to state this idea in one succinct sentence. Write this sentence or, better yet, just a phrase that describes your book on an index card. This is your "topic card." Place this card at the top, center of your storyboard. This keeps the idea in front of you so that you will remain on task and on track as your write your book. Make sure you, and anyone working with you, understand your topic. For example, I have a topic card that reads, "A book for teens about teenagers in the Bible."

STEP TWO: BRAINSTORM OBJECTIVES

Now define your objectives. Ask yourself, "What am I trying to accomplish with this book?" Write each individual idea on its own card. Pin these cards on your storyboard in a row under a card that reads "Objectives." Gather as many ideas as possible. You can go back later to combine the ones that are alike and get rid of the ones that have no relevance. Some of the objectives for my teen book are to—

- Help teens identify with Bible characters
- Surprise teens with information about biblical teens who were just like them
- Help teens make quality lifestyle choices

- Let teens know the Bible is for and about them
- Inspire teens to apply biblical principles to their daily lives
- Generate interest in Bible characters as real people
- Inspire teens to memorize Scriptures that relate to their personal situations

STEP THREE: DEFINE AUDIENCE

Now brainstorm about your audience. For whom are you writing this book? Who is your primary audience? Who is your secondary audience? Who will read this book, and who will buy this book? Gather these ideas and pin them up under a heading card that reads "Audience." The "Audience" column for my teen book partially reads like this:

- Teens, fourteen to eighteen years old
- Parents of teens who are fourteen to eighteen years old
- Sunday school teachers
- Youth pastors
- Christian schoolteachers

STEP FOUR: BRAINSTORM DISTINCTIVE CHARACTERISTICS

Now brainstorm your distinctive characteristics. What will make your book readable? How will this book be unique? What will make someone pick this book off the shelf, buy it, read it, or give it and recommend it to a friend? Here's an example of some distinctive characteristics of my teen book:

- Fun
- Short chapters
- Interactive
- Language relates to teens
- Touches real-life issues

STEP FIVE: ESTABLISH CHAPTER HEADINGS

Ask yourself or your focus group, "If you were going to buy a book about this topic, what would you expect to learn or read about? Place each idea on a separate card. The main ideas become your chapter headings; minor ideas can become chapter subheads. Be sure to then liven up your chapter titles, making them catchy with techniques such as consistently using the same part of speech or beginning each one with the same letter.

I asked my focus group for the teen book to tell me what they thought of teenagers. I then matched their thoughts with a Bible teen.

- Impulsive: David
- Lazy: the prodigal son
- Stubborn: David
- Naïve: Isaac
- Unconcerned: Mary

STEP SIX: DEVELOP CHAPTER OUTLINES

Next, storyboard your chapter outlines. Under each chapter heading, place cards that explain or describe what will be in each chapter.

IMPULSIVE DAVID
Passage: 1 Samuel 16–17
Theme: I will not run from Goliath.
Take-away: Christian teens show courage in the face of opposition to their faith.
Tell the story through the eyes of David.
Apply David's story to modern possibility of showing courage in the face of opposition to your faith.
Contemporary examples:
1. Science teacher presents theory of evolution as a fact
2. Popular kids invite you to join a club that meets on Sunday mornings.
Interactive Activity: Record comments made about God or religion on TV. Do these comments show a wrong view of God? If so, why watch the show?
Memory verse: Proverbs 3:26

STEP SEVEN: DEVELOP BOOK PROPOSAL

Once you have outlined all of your chapters, you have almost all the information you will need to draft your book proposal. Your topic card becomes your opening statement. This is what your book is about. Formulate your objectives into several sentences that will follow your opening statement. Next, in two separate paragraphs, describe your audience and explain your distinctive characteristics by using the information from these columns. Then add a paragraph telling your prospective publisher why you are the right person to write this book. The next section should contain a market analysis explaining how your book is different from others like it already on the market. Finally, write a section detailing how you are willing to help with marketing.

STEP EIGHT: DRAFT THE TABLE OF CONTENTS AND CHAPTER SYNOPSIS

Use your chapter outlines from step six to formulate your table of contents and to write your chapter synopsis. Draft succinct paragraphs detailing what each chapter will contain. Include the chapter's focus, theme, take-away, and any special features that will be included therein.

STEP NINE: WRITE YOUR QUERY LETTER

Condense the information from your proposal and chapter synopsis into a query letter to prospective publishers. This is a one-page, attention grabber that will move the acquisitions editor to be interested enough in your project to read your proposal and move it to the next step of the publishing process.

STEP TEN: DEVELOP A PLANNING STORYBOARD

Finally, develop a planning storyboard. Either based on your own personal timetable or that of your publisher, plan out how long it will take you to write your book. Once you receive a contract, you will probably have months, if not an entire year to write your book. Look ahead in your calendar and block out special dates like birthdays, anniversaries, and holidays. Then figure out how many days you have to work until your deadline. Set your finishing date two weeks before your deadline. Schedule realistically, knowing whether you will actually write every day and figuring in Murphy's Law (anything that can go wrong, will go wrong). Let the planning board act as a policeman to keep you on task. Here's an example:

Time Frame	Week 1	Week 2	Week 3	Week 4	Week 5	Week 6	Week 7
Chapter	Impulsive David		Unconcerned Mary				Naïve Isaac
Activity	Research Chapter 1	Write Chapter 1	Research Chapter 2	Write Chapter 2 (set aside) edit Chapter 1	Edit Chapter 2 Send sample chapters and full proposal to publisher	No writing, anniversary vacation	Research Chapter 3

By putting the storyboarding process into practice, you will keep yourself organized, allow others to participate in your creativity, and stay on task to meet your deadline.

IN REVIEW

—————— Sharon Norris Elliott ——————

Step One:	Define Topic
Step Two:	Brainstorm Objectives
Step Three:	Define Audience
Step Four:	Brainstorm Distinctive Characteristics
Step Five:	Establish Chapter Headings
Chapter Six:	Develop Chapter Outlines
Step Seven:	Develop Book Proposal
Step Eight:	Draft the Table of Contents and Chapter Synopsis
Step Nine:	Write Your Query Letter
Step Ten:	Develop a Planning Storyboard

16

WRITING A
FICTION BOOK

Denise Williamson

*There are three rules for writing a novel. Unfortunately no one
knows what they are.*

—W. Somerset Maugham

Somewhere along the way a novelist has detained you. Made you keep your
light on in the dead of the night. Now you want to do the same to others.
This chapter probably won't be enough to launch your career. My goal is to get
you started, while challenging you to consider honestly why you want to write
a novel.

The schoolhouse definition that says *non-fiction is true* and *fiction is not true*
has done us all a great disservice. Using facts alone, writers cannot communicate
purpose or perspective. That's why even journalists use story-telling techniques
to connect our interests with the events they write about. Conversely, novelists
know that fiction must be *believable* to be readable. Thus, they skillfully use facts
to achieve a sense of *verisimilitude*—the semblance of reality. We are, however,
more than successful literary liars!

Fellow Christian author Randy Alcorn observes that fiction can have a
"Trojan horse" effect, by which an author can catch readers unawares. "People
open the door of their minds to a story," Randy says. "The Trojan horse comes

125

in, and then, all of the sudden, the soldiers come out, and they take over the city." We can favor fiction's great influence, or nearly despise it. We like to remember that Harriet Beecher Stowe used *Uncle Tom's Cabin* to turn a nation against slavery and that Charles Dickens pricked readers' consciences about child labor. But what of the influences of a non-real boy named Harry Potter? What of the heretical philosophies of a fictitious professor in *The Da Vinci Code*?

FICTION AS ART

Fiction is art. That's why novels have tremendous influence on our senses. Art is always interpretative. Every author leaves indelible marks of her own worldview upon her fiction, just as every painter does upon his canvas. Set five landscape artists to work on the same riverbank, and you'll get five different paintings. Inspire five novelists with the same event, and you'll get five unique tales. Painting is a medium of visual interpretation. Fiction puts brushstrokes upon the heart. When you are skilled as a novelist you can replicate sights, sounds, smells, and textures. You can create vicarious experiences as you make your characters' motives transparent to your readers. Of all art forms, ours comes closest to giving others the experience of living one or more lives that are not their own. Through your words, readers can be exposed to perspectives that are new to them. When readers finish your novel, their view of reality may be permanently altered. That's a pretty weighty prospect!

In our society, truth has become subject to the "aye" of the beholder. How might the novels we write open windows onto landscapes of the Kingdom, even for some who dismiss the historic message of the Cross? As Christian artists, we need not always engage the assumed issues of faith directly. We should pen some of the best of our society's good-natured humor, romance fired by the passions of matrimonial love, suspense that calls for cunning *and* self-sacrifice. Our novels will have a genuine watermark of faith upon them when our relationship with the Author of Life as "Abba, Father" has dramatic effect upon our creativity. Tapping the power of fiction for us must first be by prayer. Add a poet's sensitivity, an investigative reporter's attention to detail, and a grammarian's understanding of language and nuance—and you're ready to begin.

THE WELLSPRINGS

You glimpse a homeless child through your windshield, touch an heirloom quilt, or hear statistics on teen suicide. These are story "starters." It may be weeks, even years, until you flesh out a novel with some of them, but make it a habit to record the ideas when they come. I've found *five* wellsprings for my fiction: an interesting *person*, An intriguing *place* (geographically or historically), a unique *prop* (such as the heirloom quilt), a compelling *plot* (inspired by real or imagined events), and a *premise* I believe in. These wellsprings feed all the rivers (or genres) of fiction: mystery, historical, suspense, science fiction, and all their common confluences, such as historical romance.

As a wordsmith, then, you must be comfortable with the skills needed to transform these resources into art. Here's a brief look at some of the basics of the novel, along with a few hands-on activities to get you writing right away.

YOUR CHARACTERS

You create interesting characters by combining thought and action, and revealing it through a mix of dialogue and narration. Readers relate to boldly formed characters who deal with heartaches, tragedies, successes, and failures that ring true to life. Your fiction may be a reader's first look into a genuinely Christ-centered life. It needs to be honest and compelling. It is possible to write fiction that perpetuates the secularist's dim view that believers are simplistic, dogmatic, defensive, and petty. Hopefully, this is not your goal. Complex characterization and creative encounters are two essentials in avoiding the shallow plot.

A personal salvation experience need not be the focal point of your work. Don't force picture-perfect endings. Too many characters diffuse the poignancy. The right interaction of characters provides great pressure points and opportunities for creative resolutions.

Pick one character from a story you love. Consider how the details of his or her life are revealed. What devices does the author use to give description? What actions are employed to reveal the character's strong and weak points? Choose one novel and write a summary of all the characters. Consider how the author facilitates the interaction of characters by the individual traits invested in each one. How does each character change or affect change in the story?

THE POWER OF POINT OF VIEW

Any close examination of character will lead you to "point of view." Your characters carry your stories, much as actors do. No one wants to see the producer on stage. No one wants to hear the author's intrusive voice. Every element of your story must convincingly emerge through and around your characters.

A "point of view" character is one who holds the live camera. Everything your readers sense or feel comes from the vicarious relationship you construct between that character and them. In juvenile fiction, the point of view character often is a child. In romance, the point of view character may be a woman with whom your readers can relate. Complex fiction usually calls for multiple viewpoints. Tensions can be heightened when readers "see" through several different sets of eyes. Multiple viewpoints most readily simulate life, for each of us truly functions within a limited worldview.

Examine a novel written in several viewpoints. Assign each viewpoint character to a different color of index card. Write down a summary of events as they are revealed from each character's perspective. When the author changes viewpoint, change the color of the card. Continue to take notes until you sense some proclivity for telling one congruent story from several points of view. Take something written from one viewpoint. Break it into two. Consider what richness and complexity can come with this change.

UNDERSTANDING PACING, PLOT, AND THE AMBIANCE

All fiction is dependent on a strong beginning, interesting developments, and a satisfying ending. The nature of your novel will determine whether you write a fast-paced *plot-driven* work or a slow-paced *character-driven* one. You may choose to work in *first person*, as though every word is being thought or spoken by your *viewpoint* character. Even when you write in *third-person* your word choice remains important, for thoughts and opinions must belong to your characters, not you. For historical novels I rely heavily on period dictionaries.

To study the relationship between pacing and plot, list everything that happens in one chapter of a novel that significantly moves the story forward. Do this with several novels, and you'll see that fast-paced fiction has the most "plot-points" per page. Train yourself to see how chapter breaks can heighten suspense. Note how often chapters end just prior to revelation.

Practice the techniques novelists use to create an ambiance appropriate for their story. Study word choice, use of dialect, and setting. With high-lighters, mark pages in novels you own. Make action verbs one color; adjectives, another; and adverbs, a third. Then color-code some of your manuscript. Does your fiction follow the master's color-scheme?

PURSUING THE PRIZE

More self-instructing ideas can be found in books, on the Web, and in writers' magazines. Keep current with your trade by reading reputable periodicals, such as *Writer's Digest*. Select resources that can help you with the basics we've covered here. Experiment with genres you like. Try writing for any age group that interests you.

According to a recent Harris Poll, Americans' favorite leisure activity *still* is reading. That's great news! While publishers depend on well-known authors to keep producing novels that sell, hope burns bright among them for finding a "debut" writer who will steal readers' hearts. Most of us take comfort in the belief that *good* fiction will find an audience.

I encourage you to test the waters as soon as you feel ready. For some, that's when the whole manuscript is in the desk drawer. For others, the search starts with an outline, a proposal, sample chapters, and a sure completion date. Your unpublished novel can have readers. Join a critique group. Attend a writers' conference that facilitates meetings with editors or writers. Attend an authors' retreat that offers "coaching." Invest in short-term mentoring with a writer you respect. Take a course with a professor who has good publishing connections. Seek honest critique in these settings, and make your manuscript better by it.

Become a student of the industry as well as the craft. Befriend bookstore owners and get the retailer's point of view. Learn about the publishers who are part of CBA (Christian Booksellers Association). Check out www.cbaonline.org and the websites of CBA companies that release novels in your genre. A trustworthy compilation of Christian book markets is available in *Sally Stuart's Christian Writers' Market Guide*.

Do you hear the call to sell your art in the secular marketplace? Information on ABA (American Booksellers Association) is available at www.BookWeb.org. Check your library for a recent bound copy of *Writer's Market* or visit www.WritersMarket.com to see how you can access their databases for a fee. I get attached to my old dog-eared market guides, in which I write copious notes regarding updates from the Web, changes in editors, new imprints, etc.

Does your novel manuscript fit a publisher's parameters? Does the publisher have a good reputation in dealing with authors? If so, then you might proceed by preparing a submission in a most professional manner, *exactly as specified*. Be succinct in your correspondence. Send it to the right editor. An editor once requested that I summarize *three* four-hundred-page historical novels on *one* page and send it to him. Though I didn't earn his company's nod, I did sell that series next time 'round, in part, because of the one painful assignment that editor extracted from me.

Getting comfortable with the network of publishers, agents, and booksellers is an essential and rewarding part of authorship. Conferences, literary groups, genre-specific groups, and author friendships are among the best ways to meet the publishing industry's "gatekeepers." Rubbing shoulders with the right "somebody" will never be enough to sell your novel. But when the right "somebody" accepts your polished proposal, reads a sample of your fiction and *likes* it, it can lead to a great partnership. Early in my career a publisher rejected one of my proposals. Later, however, when one of their editors became an agent, *she* looked *me* up because of my work. Truth is sometimes stranger than fiction.

Still interested in writing yourself into such precarious scenes? Then I encourage you to gather some friends to pray for you. Set a few one-to-three year goals, and evaluate your progress by them. A "rejection slip" with a personalized note on it can be taken as encouragement. When your critique group just can't wait to hear more, you know you're touching hearts. On the other hand, never buy into the glamorous notion that novel-writing is the end-all for every writer. *Obedience* to Christ must be our measure of success. Wherever that leads you as a writer, I cannot think of a better career plan.

NOVEL EARNINGS

—————— Denise Williamson ——————

M any of us know what it's like to have expenses outdistance royalties and advances. Here are some tried and true ways to fund your fiction, even before you see your first novel in print.

STRUCTURE A BOOK BUDGET

Create time within your weekly schedule to work on your novel. Perhaps trade time spent reading or watching TV for writing time. Create a realistic budget to cover paper, ink, some new resources, etc. If you have a family, make sure they're on the "same page" with you in designating time and money for your work.

BREAK-IN MARKETS

Traditionally periodicals have been "break-in" markets for novelists. Consider places where you can make some short-fiction sales. Wherever editors regularly use fiction, even in Sunday school curricula and youth magazines, there is a continual need for fresh material.

DOUBLE DIPPING

As a historical fiction writer, I've sold non-fiction articles on the history of maternity fashions, apple growing, and barn raisings to national magazines, while collecting information pertinent to my novels. Look for ways you can double-dip your research and turn it into cash. See if you can sell a feature to a travel editor on a place you're considering for your novel's setting. Write spin-off assignments as you gain the expertise to do your books. In addition to the paycheck, you'll profit from the credibility that comes with publishing on topics related to your fiction.

17

GHOSTWRITING

Cecil "Cec" Murphey

You must be prepared to work always without applause.

—Ernest Hemingway

"I have a great story that needs telling, but I'm not a writer."

"I'm a public speaker with more than one hundred speaking opportunities a year. People keep asking, 'Why don't you have a book?'"

Those are two typical responses of people who come to ghostwriters—to people like me. Although I write books under my own name, I've ghosted seventy books for other people. My credentials include Franklin Graham, Dr. Ben Carson, pianist Dino Karsanakas, singer B.J. Thomas, and NFL running back Shaun Alexander.

WHO NEEDS A GHOSTWRITER?

Individuals may be outstanding in their field, but they aren't able to write. For example, I've ghosted ten books on health and fitness. Sometimes, even though they could probably write the book themselves, they don't have the time or the discipline, or it's too emotionally draining as it was for Don Piper, for whom I ghosted *90 Minutes in Heaven*. Don's an excellent communicator.

When he sits at his computer to write, he's good. But he can't sit there very long because he's a man on the go.

I wrote two books for Dr. Ben Carson. As head of the Pediatric Neurosurgery Department at Johns Hopkins Hospital, he's written technical books and he's known as one of the best neurosurgeons in the world, but he's smart enough to know that mainstream writing isn't his gift.

Some people seek us because they're public speakers and need books to sell at the back of the room. Others come strictly from vanity. One man asked me to ghost for him so he could "be somebody." I turned him down. Although I felt sorry for him—he already was somebody. For him, however, the way to be important was to have my byline.

WHAT IS GHOSTWRITING?

Contracts distinguish the *writer* from the *author*. The obvious concept is that the writer becomes invisible and focuses on the author's material. For many years, publishers didn't acknowledge ghosts. They reasoned that people would not buy the book if they knew the celebrity didn't write it.

The first ghosted book I ever wrote with my name on the cover was *Gifted Hands*, published in 1990. The byline reads "Dr. Ben Carson *with* Cecil Murphey." Did that hurt sales? Hardly. The book is still in print in hardcover, trade paper, and mass paper.

The industry trend is to acknowledge ghostwriters. Many readers don't realize *with* designates the ghostwriter. If the book has two authors, publishers use *and* between their names. The most obvious reason for change is the ethical issue. If the author didn't write the book, readers have the right to know that fact. One of my ghosted books won a Gold Medallion Book Award, and the author acknowledged me for "writing a draft" of his book.

When I ghost, I feel as though I'm a therapist. I listen to the person—nonjudgmentally. My role isn't to offer opinions, but to absorb what the authors say. I'm there to grasp their ideas and shape them into readable prose.

I also feel like an interpreter because I need to get inside authors and translate their deepest feelings and strongest convictions to the printed page.

Ghostwriting is also a way to help worthy people. I've ghosted four books for Dr. Samuel Chand, one of the leaders on future trends in churches. I love working with Sam because he has important things to say, and he values my gift as a writer.

Ghostwriting includes a trust relationship. I've heard many secrets that won't go into a book, but when clients share those things, I can understand their motivation and actions.

WHAT QUALITIES DO GHOSTWRITERS NEED?

Good ghostwriters enable readers to understand their subjects. When people put down my ghosted books, especially biographies, I want them to be able to say, "I understand this person." It's more than readers learning facts and information. For example, after I read the ghosted autobiography of Reba McIntyre, I knew about her achievements, but the inner Reba remained hidden. By contrast, Sports writer Sally Jenkins wrote two books about biker Lance Armstrong. After I read them, I *knew* Lance because Sally Jenkins made him alive on the page. That's what good ghostwriters do.

Ghostwriters need to listen even when they disagree. I've ghosted books on theological issues with which I don't agree. Publishers aren't paying for my theological views (even if I'm correct), but for the celebrity's concepts. My role isn't to rectify; my role is to understand.

WHY AM I A GHOSTWRITER?

In 1981, an editor at Fleming H. Revell approached me and asked me to ghost a celebrity book. I knew my name wouldn't appear on the book. (In fact, the author never acknowledged me.) I agonized over that and asked myself, am I willing to write and not care who receives credit? After I wrestled with the question, I answered yes.

I saw ghosting as a form of ministry; it's one way I help others. Another benefit is that I've received an education by writing on topics I didn't know anything about. I ghosted two secular books about Byrd's historic trip to Antarctica in 1928–1930 by the last surviving member of that expedition. I've written about diets even though I've never been on one. I've gleaned inside information about sports. I've written about prison life, Russia under the iron curtain, addiction, and how to prevent suicide among teens.

Ghostwriting provides a way for me to grow spiritually. As I open myself to others, I understand more about myself. This isn't conscious, but the more I understand others, the more compassionate I become and I am more aware of God's grace.

I love the challenge to think like other people. I believe God gifted me to do this and has opened the doors for me to make this a significant part of my writing ministry. This ministry provides an opportunity to challenge readers' thinking, promote causes, and sometimes to enlighten the public.

Finally, I ghostwrite because it's fun; I enjoy the people for whom I work.

ADVANTAGES AND DISADVANTAGES

First, let's consider the downside. We receive no public recognition. We may receive thousands of dollars in royalties, but the celebrity is the only one people notice—even if our name is also on the book.

For example, one time I was in a hotel for a conference. Guests were able to walk around the book display. I stood about fifteen feet away and talked to a friend and a woman paused at the table. "Oh, *Gifted Hands*. I love that book!" she said to no one in particular.

"Here's the man who wrote it," my friend said.

"He did not! Ben Carson wrote that book."

My friend walked to the table, picked up a copy, and pointed to my name.

"Oh, he did, didn't he?" the woman said. "Oh, well, it was a good book anyway."

Another factor is that ghostwriters receive no publicity and no interviews. That's fine with me. When I ghostwrite, I think of the result as the celebrity's book, not mine. Not all writers agree with me.

That leads to another negative: Some celebrities can be demanding. My most difficult was a famous Christian who made me sit across from him and his secretary while he read the manuscript aloud. They discussed each sentence as if I weren't present. If either of them had questions or objected, he would turn to me and say, "Change it!" That scene took place through three drafts.

Unless stated in the contract, ghosts have no editorial rights. When we turn in the manuscript, we're finished. That's a painful time for me because I've learned to love the people for whom I've written. In some ways, for a period of months, I felt like the author's best friend. After my work is completed, I have to remind myself, "This is a business relationship. The business is finished." A few authors have kept in touch, but for most of them, a wave of nostalgia comes over me whenever I recall the wonderful relationship we experienced.

When we look at ghostwriting, the most obvious advantage is that this form of ministry pays well. In the beginning days, I received a flat fee, no matter what kind of sales the publisher made.

When we ghostwrite, most of the time, the author provides the research material, although I always read and know more about my subject than I include in a book.

Ghostwriting is a good way to establish a reputation as a writer. Several prominent writers started by writing books for others. They used that experience to learn the craft and eventually wrote their own books.

As long as there are great stories out there or needed information that individuals can't write themselves, we'll always need ghosts.

People like me.

EXCERPT FROM
I CHOOSE TO STAY:
A BLACK TEACHER REFUSES TO
DESERT THE INNER CITY

——————— Cecil Murphey ———————

I kept thinking about inner-city kids. As long as they're alive, they have a chance to turn their lives around. As long as there are teachers and leaders out there giving of ourselves, we can make changes. Sadness filled my heart when I remembered those we hadn't been able to snatch from destruction.

I wasn't the only teacher or leader. There were others—a lot of others—and each of us carried the same burden. We cared, and because we cared, it hurt deeply when we lost a child.

I kept thinking of the funerals I had been to during the past ten years—more than I wanted to remember. Some of those we buried were young—elementary and middle school kids who happened to be playing in the wrong place when a fight broke out.

When I was a boy, I had gone to funerals—but they were only for old people. I'd stare at their lined faces and gray hair and it felt peaceful. They had lived their lives, but these kids were eight, ten, or fourteen years old. They'd never know what life really is. Too many inner-city kids grew up too fast—if they grew up—seeing the harshness of life on the streets every day. We had been a poor family, but I hadn't seen or been through what so many of those kids went though every day.

I thought of Anwar and his mother's drug problems. They had beat the neighborhood pressure, but his mother had fled to Lancaster to do so. I thought of Denise and the struggle she lived with every day, and her mom still wasn't doing well. There was Nathan who longed for a relationship with his father that seemed as if it would never develop. And there was Demetrius, who lived a thousand miles away from his mom—in his third house in two years.

I kept saying to myself, the world is larger than north Philadelphia and bigger than the ghettos. Education is their passport to another world. As I drove toward the university, I vowed afresh that I would give every child a passport to go wherever he or she wanted to go.

I know I'm impacting lives and careers—and that's encouraging, but I'm just one person. My mind kept going back to those kids who wouldn't ever stand where Otis would stand today. They'd never graduate from college.

For the ten-year period beginning in 1990, I mentally ticked off twenty of my former students who had been murdered. That's something I never thought about when I was studying to be a teacher. No education classes had ever mentioned coping with such grief.

One day on the morning news, I wept when the TV showed pictures of two of my former students. They knew each other and were in the same house when a robbery took place. Both died there.

That morning had been one of the first times that I had thought about whether I wanted to continue teaching. I didn't like that feeling of loss and ongoing pain. Each time I'd hear or read of a murdered child, I'd ask, "How can I go through this again?"

Too many funerals.

I Choose to Stay: A Black Teacher Refuses to Desert the Inner City by Salome Thomas-EL with Cecil Murphey (New York: Kensington, 2003), pages 300–302.

18

SELF-EDITING FICTION

Karen Ball

First drafts are for learning what your novel or story is about.

—Bernard Malamud

eadlines.

We all have 'em. For some they're a blessing, motivating us to set all those goals: words per day, pages per week, chapters per month, and so on. For others (and I fall in this camp), they're a bane, a guillotine blade hanging over my head as each day ticks by. Either way, with publishers pushing to get books out faster and sooner, it seems those dreaded deadlines are growing ever closer together. And that, my friends, is not good news. Because too many of us end up writing to the deadline, determined to meet it (or to miss it by as few days as humanly possible), rather than writing to ensure our craft is the strongest it can be. Some of us are barely finishing the writing before we turn the manuscripts in. Yes, that can work out fine, thanks to eagle-eyed editors and the gift of revision time. But are we giving our readers our best writing?

Too often, the answer is no.

So, what can we do about this tension? Well, the best solution is to take more time in the writing process. But if that isn't feasible, then at least take some time for a solid self-edit. Yes, editors get paid for shaping and refining your manuscript. But you, as the writer, need to make refining your craft as much a focus as meeting a deadline.

Following are the Lucky Seven: seven editing checkpoints to help you ensure your story is crafted as well as possible. Of course, your writing may be just fine without following the following . . . er, uh . . . well, you know what I mean. But I think most of us will find our writing is strengthened when we take the time for a self-edit run.

One caveat before we start: When you write, just *write*. Don't let your internal editor out to play until you're done writing. If you try to edit and write at the same time, you'll drive yourself even crazier than normal.

To help demonstrate the following points, we're going to call on two friends, Sheau Dontell and Noah DeVerbe, both avid students of fiction writing.

CHECKPOINT ONE

Only use speaker attributions when absolutely necessary. When is that? When you have more than one speaker, so the reader may confuse who is saying what, or when you have a run of dialogue that goes more than a few lines. Such as,

Sheau pulled his desk close to Noah's. "Did you bring your notes from last week?"

"Sure. They're right here."

"Great. I forgot mine, and we need to do a quick review."

"We? What? You got a mouse in your pocket?"

"Very funny."

"I thought so."

As you can see, it gets hard after awhile to keep straight who's saying what. So the edit would be as follows:

Sheau pulled his desk close to Noah's. "Did you bring your notes from last week?"

"Sure. They're right here."

"Great. I forgot mine, and we need to do a quick review."

"We?" Noah frowned. "What? You got a mouse in your pocket?"

"Very funny."

"I thought so."

One more note about attributions: make sure they're not physical impossibilities. For example, *"I thought so," he smiled.* Nope, wrong. You can't smile, grin, or grimace words. Speaking is a *verbal* act, and attributions need to be verbal actions as well (e.g., whisper, yell, call, etc.). However, most editors will tell you that just using "said" is best. It's almost invisible to the reader's eye, and that's what you want—writing that draws attention to the story, not to itself. So when you need a speaker attribution, it's best to stick to the basics.

CHECKPOINT TWO

Let your dialogue speak for itself. Make sure your speaker attributions, aren't telling readers what emotions your characters are experiencing rather than showing them through dialogue or action. Here are some examples of how *not* to do it. Sheau reads Noah's notes referring to the horrors of telling and turns to his friend:

"Telling?" he asked, confused. "What does that mean?"

or

"Telling?" he asked, his face filled with confusion. "What does that mean?"

or

"Telling," he asked, feeling confused. "What does that mean?"

Insert sound of game show buzzer here! All of the above are wrong, wrong, and . . . you guessed it, wrong! Remember, the power of fiction is that we pull the reader in for a vicarious experience. When you tell about emotions rather than showing, the reader stays at arm's length from the story and characters, and that's a major problem.

But the *confused, with confusion,* and *feeling confused* aren't the only problems here. You don't need "he asked." The question mark shows he's asking a question, so the attribution is not only telling, but redundant. It's far better to drop the speaker attribution unless it's really needed to show who is speaking. And to show the confusion with a beat.

What, you may ask, is a beat? It's action interspersed in the midst of dialogue. And the beauty of beats is that they not only replace telling and unnecessary speaker attributions, but they also help give readers more of a sense of place, action, and characters. So an edit of the telling lines could be as follows:

"Telling?" A frown pinched his brows together. "What's that?"

A helpful tip on dialogue: read it out loud. Many writers end up with dialogue that's too formal (unless, of course, you're writing about formal people in a bygone era), but we can't tell just by reading that we've fallen into that trap. So read it out loud. You'll be surprised how different it sounds—and, sometimes, how bad. If you find yourself tempted to change your dialogue after you read it aloud, give in. Not all temptation is bad!

CHECKPOINT THREE

Don't let the dreaded *-ly* adverbs get your story down! Most adverbs just don't belong, not in speaker attributions or text.

For example, Noah is reading Sheau's story, which he's written for their next class. Upon reaching a section that does *everything* wrong, Noah reacts as follows:

"I'll never write as ridiculously as that," said Noah emphatically.

Oooo, bad form, Noah ol' chap! Not one, but *two* missteps here. First, both adverbs (*ridiculously* and *emphatically*) should be exterminated. Get rid of 'em. Don't tell us Noah is disdainful of his buddy's writing, or that he's being emphatic. *Show* these things in dialogue, actions, or expressions.

As for the second misstep, "said Noah" is an antiquated format for speaker attributions. It should be "Noah said," not the other way around.

So, how should the above be edited? Simple:

A sneer touched Noah's thin lips. "I'll never write like that!"

Voilà! The beat shows he's disdainful; the exclamation point shows he's emphatic. (For even more emphasis, you could italicize the last word.)

CHECKPOINT FOUR

Watch out for words that weaken!

Noah hands his story to Sheau. "I'm really certain you'll find my story extremely well written and very different from yours."

Ummm, no. I know it's hard, but 99.99 percent of the time, it's best to just say no to superlatives and modifiers (*very, quite, extremely, super, really,* etc.) Unless, of course, such things are part of a character's personality—for example, a character who is always exaggerating or is a drama queen. But if you do that, be sure to keep those particular traits to just that one character.

CHECKPOINT FIVE

Don't be done unto. Avoid the passive voice. Passive voice is a more archaic form of writing. But what's worse is what the term implies: passive. Passive writing is weaker writing. Powerful fiction is active, immediate, and full of energy. So, rather than,

Sheau grabbed the story of Shaun's and threw it.

You make the action more immediate with,

Sheau grabbed Noah's story and threw it.

CHECKPOINT SIX

Just the facts, ma'am! Don't use exposition in either dialogue or narrative if there's no real reason to share the information. We read and research so much when writing fiction, and we discover a *lot* of neat things—especially when writing historical fiction. But make sure you only include the information that's necessary to your story for plot advancement, character development, or creating a strong sense of place. For example:

Noah stared at Sheau. "Look, I know you're upset, but showing rather then telling is an important facet of writing fiction well. Most authorities on writing fiction, including Sol Stein, Renni Browne and Dave King, and Robert McKee, speak out against telling."

Anyone asleep yet? Sure, those of us who've studied the craft know all that. But is it necessary to the story? No. So don't include it unless you need it.

CHECKPOINT SEVEN

Strong hooks. Don't leave home—or a chapter or even a scene—without 'em. Hooks keep the pages turning; they create a sense of anticipation, dread, excitement, fear, or whatever. A solid hook can be positive *or* negative (something that makes people laugh or creates a sense of impending doom), but whatever you use, it should keep such momentum going that the reader can't bear to put the book down.

Well, there you have 'em, the Lucky Seven. Using these checkpoints during your self-edit of your writing may well help you discover patterns you need to break, which will benefit not only you as a writer, but your readers. And isn't that, after all, what we're all about? Writing stories that engage, move, and change readers with the power of God's truth.

Now, have at it—and have fun!

EXCERPT FROM
THE BREAKING POINT

―――――――― Karen Ball ――――――――

R enee Roman leaned her forehead against the cold glass of the truck window, her teeth clenched, a barrier against the tears scalding the backs of her eyes. She would not cry. She'd cried enough for a lifetime.

Two lifetimes.

She focused on the winter storm screaming just outside her window. A dense blanket of wind-whipped snow surrounded the pickup as they crept along. Visibility was nil, and gusts of wind buffeted the truck, slamming against it with seemingly determined efforts to knock them sideways.

A whiteout. How fitting. Now they could be as blind to the road as they were to each other . . .

Hurt tugged at her, and she pressed her lips tight against it. Blind or not, nothing was going to stop them, no siree. Let the storm rage; their truck would still keep its steady, slow progress. Wind and snow were no match for Gabe. Nothing stopped with him when he was determined—no human, no natural disaster, no act of God . . .

Renee's fingers curled around her seat belt. Here they were, on a treacherous road, at the mercy of the weather, and all Gabe could do was keep moving forward. No stopping to reconsider, no looking for shelter, and certainly no asking for help. Just push your way through and make everything and everyone bend to *your* will.

If she weren't so terrified, the situation would be hilarious.

A small whine drew her attention to the backseat, and she turned to place a comforting hand on Bo's furry head. Funny—Siberian huskies looked so imposing, so fierce, but under that wolflike appearance, they were serious wimps. "It's okay, boy." She uttered the soothing words, doing her best to keep her own anxiety from tainting her tone. "You're fine. We'll be home soon."

If only she believed that. A glance told Renee that Gabe was tense, too, but she knew his tight jaw had little to do with the weather. She buried her fingers in Bo's thick coat. If only she could bury her feelings as completely.

I hate him.

The words, which had nudged her heart and mind since that morning despite her stubborn refusal to grant them entrance, finally took wing.

She knew it was because of the anger. And the terror. She hated driving in the snow. Usually avoided it at all costs—which put driving in a blinding blizzard in the Oregon mountains in the "Things I Utterly Detest" category—but Gabe had been adamant. And nothing she said—no pleas to wait a day, no appeals to reason or compassion—had made a difference.

Excerpt from The Breaking Point *by Karen Ball,*
Multnomah Publishing, Inc., 2002

19

SELF-EDITING NONFICTION

Julie-Allyson Ieron

*The beautiful part of writing is that you don't have to get it
right the first time, unlike, say, a brain surgeon.*

—Robert Cormier

One of my first paying jobs as a real-live writer was as a contributor to a daily devotional guide. When I received the initial assignment, my excitement at being paid to do what I loved was beyond words. Then I began to study the unforgiving parameters of the format. And I do mean unforgiving. I had to count number of lines (23) and number of letters on each line (42–51, including punctuation and spaces). I had to be sure to include a two-line Scripture up top and a two- or three-line prayer at the close. My title needed to be short and to the point. And it all needed a one-line wrap-up to leave an impression on the readers and offer something uplifting to take them through the day. All of this was in the pre-computer days, when retyping after each edit was a necessary evil.

How did I keep this freelancing job for more than five years? Early on, I chose to make the process of editing my friend. Most often, I would write long—much longer than I could cram into the template. Then I would get out the machete. Cut. Cut. Cut. To my amazement, the devotions I clipped and polished were infinitely stronger than those I would attempt to prepare using the lazy shortcut of writing to fit the count exactly on the first pass.

Write long-long-long and trim-trim-trim. It's a lesson I've carried with me from that day to this, and it has had a powerful impact on my finished prose.

GOING TO SCHOOL ON STORYTELLERS

A few years ago, one of my clients asked me to edit a book by professional storyteller John Walsh. I enjoyed the experience of helping John turn his rough manuscript into a polished book that continues to sell well. Not only did I get to teach John a few things about publishing, but he also taught me valuable lessons about storytelling that I've since been able to translate to my own self-editing.

In oral storytelling, tellers often don't consider a story "ready" for prime time until they have told it one hundred times. Yes, I said *one hundred*. Not five or ten. A full one hundred. And yet, as I write, I am tempted to think I have reached never-to-be-improved-upon perfection on the first pass. John taught me a great lesson about telling stories on paper—refining and editing and refining some more does nothing but strengthen my communication.

What is editing, after all? I define it as taking pass after pass through a rough piece of writing until it has reached a level of refinement approaching perfection.

The first passes I make with my machete, heartlessly killing whole sentences or paragraphs that don't fit with the piece's purpose. If I am too in love with my words at this stage, I create a computer file where I can cut and paste sections that I can't bear to send to cyberspace oblivion. I seldom return to this file, but I am more willing to do the best for a manuscript if I'm not obsessing about precious words being gone forever. Next, I get out a pocketknife to trim out words and phrases that get in the way. Finally, I get out a chamois to do the final polishing for cadence and grammar.

ON THE ART SIDE

Editing has within it elements of both art and science. Let me explain.

The great Renaissance sculptor Michelangelo said that when he looked at a block of marble, he saw an image locked inside. His job was to free the majestic *David* or the emotive *Pieta* from all the extraneous stone that was blocking it from sight. This imaginative process is one I've taken to heart as a writer. As I look at a blank screen or a clean piece of paper, I see what it can become: what message it can convey to a reader, and what life-changing impact it can have. I work to unlock that message—to free it from anything that would block it from a reader's sight.

HONE OUT REDUNDANCIES

Some of the earliest chunks of unnecessary stone I remove are redundancies, which I define as words or phrases that take up more room than they need to. For example, "dog puppies" should become simply "puppies," unless we're talking about some animal other than a dog having puppies. "Due to the fact that" becomes "because." "Absolutely sure" becomes "sure." "Foresee the future" becomes "foresee." You get the idea.

HONE OUT CLICHÉS

Next, I hunt for clichés—those phrases that were once clever but now have become overused. Clichés are the lazy way to tell a story. God gave each of us a creative mind with a unique point of view. He calls on us to use that creativity to find a fresh turn-of-phrase that makes readers think about the subject in a way they've never done before. A cliché can't do that because it's expected and ordinary.

In doing this kind of trimming, often (not "quite often," which I was tempted to write—just "often") we're able to free up space to add pertinent points or fresh examples.

ADD ILLUSTRATIONS

So, once I've cut redundancies and clichés, I have room to add stories that illustrate my points—stories that take abstract concepts and turn them into concrete scenes that have relevance in the reader's life.

For example, in one of the early lessons in the Christian Writers Guild apprentice curriculum, an assignment asks students to give their salvation testimony. Invariably, most students will write that they "came to Christ." But they don't show what that means. So, I ask for a rewrite by noting in the margin,

"Show, don't tell." I'll encourage them to put this abstract concept into words that are so well explained and described that any reader (a seeker or a skeptic) will know exactly how to "come to Christ." They might come back with an edit that reads, "I realized I was hopeless in my sin (I just cut the words "that" and "really" from this sentence because neither was carrying its weight). As I read John 3:16, I saw that God sent Jesus to solve my sin problem. He lived and died to offer me forgiveness and to make a way for me to have an ongoing relationship with his Father, God. So, I prayed to acknowledge my sin and ask Jesus to forgive me and save me from its consequences. He did. And now I have the privilege of being a child of God."

Yes, concrete example stories do take up more words than a quick telling of the abstract concept. But they add color and vivid life. More importantly, they tell the readers what they need to know.

CHECK FOR CADENCE

On my final pass through my manuscripts, I often read them aloud. In this reading I not only see typographical errors I've glossed over previously, but I'm also able to listen for cadence. Have I used too many long sentences in a row (these lull readers into monotony)? Or have I used too many short sentences in a row (these put readers into a fevered pace that will exhaust them)? Varying the cadence will provide a more pleasing experience for the reader.

ON THE SCIENCE SIDE

Now that we've used our machetes and our pocketknives, it's time for the chamois. I use this polishing tool to undertake a less glamorous, more scientific task in the editing process. On this science side is one dreaded word: grammar. For you, it may conjure up fearsome scenes of diagramming sentences and conjugating verbs. But poor grammar is one more chunk of that ugly, rough stone that blocks our communication.

If we're choosing to write in English, there are facts about the language that we'll need to know and use to our advantage. Which words get placed in which part of a sentence? How do we punctuate a sentence for maximum clarity? Where will a phrase get the most punch and attention? Which verb and which pronoun is correct in the context? Our word processor's grammar checker can help here, but it is insufficient. We need to know the facts ourselves to be able to use them most effectively.

If you've studied a non-English language, you'll recall that these facts change from language to language. When I was a child, I had a friend whose first language wasn't English. I can still remember a sentence she used that sent me into hysterics: "Throw me down the stairs my shoes." In her language, this was the proper structure to ask for her shoes to be thrown down the stairs. But, as you've already recognized, when stated this way in English, it sounds like she is asking her shoes to throw her down the stairs.

A FINAL CHALLENGE

Remember that unforgiving daily devotional format I described at the beginning of this chapter? I'd challenge you to take one of your own articles, perhaps an inspirational piece, and try to fit it into that format using all of the editing tools you've now acquired. You'll be surprised at how much you can say to a reader using a few precise words. I guarantee it's an exercise that will pay dividends whether you write brief articles or voluminous tomes.

A Self-Editing Checklist

————— James N. Watkins —————

LIMIT YOUR MESSAGE
- Write a three-word summary of your article or book.
- Delete *everything* that doesn't *directly* and *naturally* relate to your three-word summary.

LIMIT YOUR AUDIENCE
- Have a precise vision for whom you are writing. (Don't write for everyone!)
- Know that audience.

ORGANIZE YOUR MESSAGE
- **CASE HISTORY**
  1. Create a problem.
  2. Have an anecdote of the problem's solution.
  3. Explain precisely how it was solved.
  4. Prove the solution.
  5. Challenge the reader to participate in the solution.

- **HARD NEWS**
  1. Include the five *w*'s and an *h* (who, what, where, when, why, how) in the first paragraph.
  2. Put less important information in the following paragraphs, with each paragraph decreasing in importance.

- **PERSONALITY STORY**
  1. Illustrate the person's personality with a lead anecdote.
  2. Give the person's present status (who, what, and where the person is).

3. Have a big "flashback" (how person arrived at present state).

4. Give a closing anecdote (complete the "circuit").

- **PERSUASIVE ARTICLE**

Pure logic (rhetoric)	Popular logic (media)
1. State problems.	1. Recommend solution.
2. Review facts.	2. State problem.
3. Review possible solutions.	3. Give supporting reasons.
4. Recommend one solution.	4. Review facts.
5. Give supporting reasons.	5. Review possible solutions.
6. Spell out likely effects.	6. Spell out likely effects.

- **SELF-HELP**

1. Give an anecdote of person(s) in need of help.

2. Provide steps to the solution, with anecdotes for each point.

3. Give an anecdote or testimony of an over-comer ("You can too!").

- **TREND PIECE**

1. Create a Lead (shocking facts, profile, etc.).

2. Give a description of present status.

3. Provide an explanation of causes.

4. Make an evaluation.

5. Give a forecast or possible consequences.

ADVERTISE YOUR MESSAGE

- Attract attention with your *very first* paragraph.
- Establish the subject and tone of the article.
- Lead *naturally* into the article or story with your first paragraph.

PRESENT YOUR MESSAGE CLEARLY AND SIMPLY

- Use the best words (big difference between lightning *bug* and lightning *bolt*).

    1. Use easily understood words ("write to express, not impress").

2. Use specific words (not "dessert," but "Oreo mint chocolate chip sundae").

3. Use picture nouns and action verbs (avoid adverbs and adjectives).

4. Use only *absolutely, necessary* words.

5. Use a variety of words (make sure they're "easily understood").

- Use clear, clean, concise sentences.

  1. Have one idea per sentence.

  2. Use short sentences (aim for fifteen words maximum).

  3. Vary sentence lengths.

- Use manageable paragraphs.

  1. Have one idea per paragraph.

  2. Use short paragraphs (aim for five to seven lines maximum).

  3. Vary paragraph lengths.

- Use transitions between sentences, paragraphs, and sections. These can be:

  1. Single words (furthermore, meanwhile, nevertheless, therefore, consequently, etc.)

  2. Key words repeated throughout the article/book

  3. Time and locale ("Later that day, as he checked into the hotel . . .")

  4. Mood changes ("Her smile twisted into a frown as . . .")

  5. Changes in viewpoint ("But many disagree with that position, arguing that . . .")

  6. Numbered points

THE BUSINESS

20

PROFESSIONALISM

Bob Hostetler

No man but a blockhead ever wrote except for money.

—Samuel Johnson

There are two kinds of writers in the world. Both are valid. Both deserve respect. But they write from vastly different starting points and critically disparate perspectives. They are the hobbyist and the professional.

Hobbyists write what they want to write. Sounds simple, right? It is. Hobbyists generally approach the writing task for the enjoyment of coming up with a clever idea and writing it well. They write primarily for enjoyment. They tend to sit down at the desk or computer thinking, "Let's have some fun," or "Let's see where this goes," or "Let's try something new." That's all good stuff, of course, and often reaps wonderful results. But it's not the way professionals approach the writing task.

SELL IT BEFORE YOU WRITE IT

Professionals don't typically start a new piece of writing at the same place as hobbyists, who simply write what they want to write. Professionals write what others want to read. That's a critical difference. Professionals who are writing for publication start not in the writer's mind, but in the reader's mind. And they write, not primarily for enjoyment, but for effect. The operative question for the professional is not, "What do I feel like writing?" but "What is my reader (or editor) interested in?"

Of course, those of us just starting out in writing for publication don't yet have readers. We may not have a handle on what readers and editors are looking for. So how do we learn to think like a professional? How do we make the transition from hobbyist to professional? Two words: query letters.

SELL IT WITH A QUERY LETTER

Query letters are among the most valuable tools of writing professionals. Yet they are perhaps the most neglected by aspiring writers. That's why at writers' conferences I often spend a good deal of time teaching what I consider the top ten benefits of using a good query letter as a professional writing tool.

IT BRANDS YOU INSTANTLY AS A PROFESSIONAL

Amateurs don't write query letters, primarily because amateurs don't know what a query letter is or how to write one (see sidebar for a quick primer). Even if they're familiar with the term, they seldom understand its value as a professional writing and marketing tool. Thus, by sending a first-rate query letter to an editor, you introduce yourself as a professional. You immediately set yourself apart from the vast, unwashed writing masses.

IT FORCES YOU TO FOCUS YOUR IDEA BEFORE YOU WRITE

As a part-time hobbyist and full-time professional, I know that when I sit down to write for fun, I don't need a plan. But when I write for publication, a sharp focus is absolutely critical if I'm going to deliver quality work. Occasionally the first few drafts of a query letter seem stilted, or rambling, or unexciting. That's usually due to a lack of focus.

Later, however, as I work on it, and refine the idea, and focus it so that it can't fail to find its mark in an editor's heart and mind, it becomes vibrant, alive. So, when I write a query letter, I'm applying a discipline to my writing that will pay off abundantly when I later sit down to write the manuscript.

IT HELPS YOU DECIDE WHICH WRITING IDEAS TO PURSUE

Aspiring writers often ask me, "I have three or four really good ideas. How do I decide which one I should write first?" I usually explain that writers who use query letters as marketing tools never have to ask that question. They can develop each idea as much as a query letter will require, and then send them out and let the market decide. I've known too many writers who have spent years honing a book manuscript that never had a chance. If they had queried their ideas first, they would have learned through the process which ideas would fly and which probably would not.

IT SAVES YOU FROM WRITING "UN-SELLABLE" STUFF

When I started writing full-time in 1993, I determined that if I was going to support my wife and two children with my writing income, I could no longer afford to write anything that didn't sell. Since that time, I've sold virtually everything I've written, primarily because I've used query letters to get an assignment—or at least a good "nibble"—from an editor before further developing any idea.

IT ENLISTS THE MOST QUALIFIED PEOPLE (EDITORS) INTO YOUR CRITIQUE CIRCLE

Aspiring writers often crave feedback on their ideas and skills, but they have trouble enlisting quality critique. Critique is always a good idea, and I suggest to beginning writers that they never send anything to an editor that hasn't been thoroughly critiqued by several other people. But in addition to the critique that a writers' group or an e-mail critique circle can supply, using query letters as a professional writing and marketing tool can actually enlist real, live editors into your critique circle. If you take seriously even the slightest comments from an editor, such as, "We prefer a more conversational tone," or "Thanks, but the plot isn't quite strong enough," you can learn from the best in the business.

IT ALLOWS YOU TO SLANT AND SCULPT THE WRITING ACCORDING TO AN EDITOR'S SPECIFICATIONS

Editors will occasionally respond to a query letter with a (sometimes handwritten) note such as, "Send the manuscript, but make sure you include examples from our denomination," or "Yes, let's see it, but keep it broad; we have another writer developing a related piece on some of the specifics." Editorial direction like that is invaluable because it increases your chances of nailing the assignment.

IT GETS A QUICKER RESPONSE THAN A MANUSCRIPT

When I was a magazine editor, manuscripts and correspondence were handled differently. Manuscripts went atop a tall stack of previous submissions (the "slush pile," in editorial parlance). Letters were opened and placed directly on my desk. Manuscripts could take weeks, even a couple months, to handle during our busiest times. A query letter could be responded to in a fraction of the time and sometimes even turned around in a single day!

IT IS EASIER TO FOLLOW UP ON A REJECTION

There's an entirely different psychology at work inside me when dealing with the "rejection" of an idea I've queried, compared to what it used to be like when I sent full manuscripts for an editor's consideration. When an editor rejected my manuscript, it felt like he or she was rejecting my work, my writing, sometimes even me (though I realized when I became an editor that he or she was more likely rejecting my lack of knowledge of the publication!).

But when an editor turns down an idea I've queried, it's the idea that's being rejected, not me or my work. That's one reason why I find it easier to follow up on a "no-thank-you" response to a query letter. I don't have to spend days and days laboring over another manuscript; I simply have to come up with another great idea—maybe one that's a little more appropriate for this particular market—and send it to the same editor (often with a few words of thanks for the kind way in which he or she responded to my earlier query).

IT GIVES YOU A JUMP ON THE WRITING PROCESS

Because I put a lot of effort into the "hook" of a query letter (see sidebar), I often discover when I sit down to write the manuscript that I've already written my lead. (After all, gold is gold, right?). Sometimes, because I've detailed the main points of the piece in my "nuts and bolts" paragraph, I also realize that I've outlined the body of the article. And more than once, the "why me?" paragraph has been supplied as a "bio blurb" at the end of a finished article, or to the design or marketing department for use on the back cover of a book. Not always, of course, but more often than not, the process of writing the query letter ends up giving me a running start when I need it most.

IT ALLOWS YOU TO WRITE "REQUESTED MATERIAL" ON YOUR SUBMITTED MANUSCRIPT

When your query letter results in an editor's invitation to submit a manuscript (or, better yet, an assignment), you have the luxury of bypassing the slush pile entirely by writing (in big letters) on the lower left corner of the submission envelope, "REQUESTED MATERIAL." This advantage cannot be overestimated. Just as the query letter branded you as a professional at the beginning of the process, those two words on your submission cue the editor to prioritize your work, as it is clearly something he or she has already evaluated and invited.

Of course, even with these advantages, the use of a query letter is no guarantee of success in writing for publication. But in teaching hundreds of aspiring writers both the art and the advantage of a good query letter, I've seen some who take the challenge and determine to adopt this mark and tool of the professional writer . . . and some who don't. It's the former group whose bylines appear regularly in the magazines and books I buy and read.

A QUICK PRIMER ON A QUALITY QUERY

 Bob Hostetler

Whole books have been written to teach aspiring writers how to write a single-spaced, one-page query letter. There is certainly a lot of work and expertise that goes into a great query. It should be your best work. It should be given as much care and critique as the masterpiece it is designed to sell.

But it's not terribly complicated. It is a one-page letter, addressed like any business letter, to an editor, by name. Never address a query letter only to "Submissions Editor" or "Acquisitions Editor." If a reliable, current market guide doesn't list the appropriate editor's name, call the company and learn the name of the current editor, along with the proper mode of address (Mr., Mrs., Miss).

Of course, it's the body of the letter that will sell—or sink—the idea. In my writers' conference workshops, I encourage aspiring writers to focus their efforts on creating three strong but simple paragraphs:

THE HOOK

Every query letter needs a gripping lead or "hook," to interest the editor in your idea. If you're querying fiction, it may be a striking scene or setup from your story, or a snippet of dialogue that is central to the plot. In the case of nonfiction, the hook can be a list, a striking quote, a series of questions, or an impacting illustration, like my "hook" for the book, *The New Tolerance*:

> The Borg.
> Half human, half machine. A highly advanced race of predators. They seduce individuals with sophisticated mind control and eventually assimilate their victims into "the Collective," a single group mind in which all individual thought, action, and personality are lost.... They have no conscience. No ethic. And they will not stop until they have destroyed or assimilated all their enemies.

The Borg is fictional, of course, the ingenious creation of the minds behind the popular *Star Trek* television and movie series. But it has its counterpart in contemporary culture. Chances are, it has already infiltrated your community, your schools, your church . . . even your children.

NUTS AND BOLTS

The second paragraph of your query letter gives your idea a title and describes it as effectively as possible (e.g., "a 1,500-word how-to article, entitled 'Quilting Your Way to Mental Health,' that will not only detail the mental health benefits of quilting for your readers, but will help them get started quickly, easily, and affordably"). This paragraph should read like ad copy: snappy, bright, and descriptive.

WHY ME?

The final paragraph of your query letter simply explains why you're the perfect person to write the piece. Beginning writers often think they're at a disadvantage at this point because they have no prior publishing credits. But while you can certainly mention a few impressive credits if you have them, the best information to offer in this paragraph is often related not to writing but to the subject you're writing about (like your passion for quilting, for instance—*and* twenty years trying to regain your mental health!).

Just three paragraphs. That may not seem like much. But if you pack each of those paragraphs with a punch, it may just be enough to score a knockout.

21

RIGHTS AND COPYRIGHTS

Sally Stuart

The free-lance writer is a man who is paid per piece or per word or perhaps.

—Robert Benchley

In 1978, when the current copyright law went into effect, my writing career was starting to take off, so I was interested in what the law had to say. I decided to send for a copy of the new law, read up on it, and be prepared to go on with my writing. When the copy arrived, I was more than a little surprised that it came in a large folder and was over an inch think. So much for that quick read.

Fortunately I soon found out that there was only a small portion of the law that actually affected me directly as a writer. It was important that I was familiar with that portion, but I didn't have to worry about the rest of it. It's that applicable portion we'll discuss in this chapter.

One of the most important things you need to know is what the various rights are that you can sell or you will be asked to sell to your work. That information is explained in the sidebar to this article, called "Know What Rights You Are Selling." I would encourage you to spend some time memorizing the various rights so you are knowledgeable enough to understand and protect your rights when dealing with editors.

Now, let's look at some of the elements of the copyright law that you will need to be aware of and need to understand as they apply to your writing projects.

THE BASICS

The current law went into effect January 1, 1978, and applies only to what was published on or after that date. Actually, everything you write has automatic copyright protection from the time it reaches a fixed form (you have it out of your head and written down on a notepad or hard drive) and it then becomes your personal property. The copyright isn't registered (we'll talk about that later), but you do control when and how it can be used. If you have a co-author in the work, you own the copyright jointly. If you contribute to a collective work, your story or chapter will be copyrighted separately from the rest of the book.

COPYRIGHT NOTICE

When this law took effect in 1978, it required that your copyright notice be on the piece in order to be protected, and that stipulation remained until March 1, 1989, when that part of the law was amended to say the notice was no longer needed for protection. However, to avoid confusion it is recommended that you still include a copyright notice on each piece of writing. If the copyright notice is on the piece, there is no chance someone would assume it was in public domain and feel free to use it without permission.

The copyright notice needs to be prepared to fit an established format of three parts. That would include the copyright symbol ©, the word Copyright, or the abbreviation Copr.; the year of first publication or creation; and the author's name. You may put the copyright notice on unpublished as well as published works.

DURATION OF COPYRIGHT

Anything you wrote after January 1, 1978, is protected from the date of creation to a date 70 years after your death. If you have a co-author, it is until 70 years following the death of the last surviving author. If you created the piece anonymously or wrote it under a pseudonym, the work is protect for 95 years after publication or 120 years after creation, whichever is shorter. If your material was written prior to January 1, 1978, the original copyright is extended to a maximum total of 95 years.

Note that the current copyright law does not restore copyright protection to any works already in the public domain. Going into public domain is what happens to a work that was never copyrighted (prior to 1978), or for which the copyright has already expired. Once in public domain, the public is free to quote from it without having to ask permission (although you do still give credit to the author). In essence, it then belongs to the public—not to the author. Most government publications are not copyrighted, so they are good sources for research that does not require you to ask permission.

FAIR USE

One of the most common questions that comes up concerning copyright is "When do I have to ask permission to quote from someone else's writings?" The answer to that question is closely tied to an understanding of "fair use." Unfortunately the law itself does not lay out an easy-to-follow definition of how much you can and cannot quote without asking permission. However, it does lay out four criteria to take into consideration when making that determination.

1. The character of the use, including whether it is for commercial or nonprofit use. (Is the use going to result in some income to you, or is no profit involved? It's more likely to be fair if it's nonprofit.)

2. The amount of material used in relation to the work as a whole. (Have you pulled out the essence of the work or just incidental portions, such as an anecdote? Many publishers will allow up to one hundred words or one-tenth of the total work. You will still need to provide proper attribution.)

3. The nature of the copyrighted work, including how it is typically used. (Are you quoting a paragraph from an article or two pages from a three-volume set?)

4. The effect your use of the material is going to have on the potential market for or value of the copyrighted work. (If it diminishes the value, then the use is not fair.)

Since the fair-use provisions don't lay out a clear path for the author, I recommend that you study the four criteria above and then use your common sense to ask if it is fair use. You can also ask yourself if you would want to be asked for permission if the quotes in question came from your work. You do always need permission to quote something in its entirety—such as a full article, story, or poem.

ASKING PERMISSION

The next question then is, "How do I get permission for those quoted passages?" If the quote comes from a book, check the copyright page to see if the book is copyrighted in the name of the author or the publisher. If in the name of the publisher, write them directly to ask permission. If in the name of the author, write the author and mail the letter to the publisher, asking them to forward it to the author. They aren't likely to release the author's address to you.

When seeking permission for any use, you need to be very specific about what you are asking for. They will need to know how you will be using the material, and the exact quote you want to use (starting with this phrase on page x and ending with this phrase on page y). If it's going into a book, ask for permission for this book, plus all future revisions and editions, and nonexclusive world rights in all languages. That way you don't have to come back and ask permission for each new edition.

REGISTRATION

If you get protection for your work without actually registering it, then why would you register it? In most cases you won't. The only value there is in a registered copyright is that it gives you the right to sue someone for infringing on your copyright (likely quoting from it without permission or without giving you credit). If we are talking about articles, unless you were paid top rates for those pieces, there usually is not enough money involved to justify a suit. Even with a book, unless someone has made it into a movie or infringed on the merchandising rights, there still isn't enough money at stake.

If you register before or within five years of publication, you have established the validity of your copyright in case you want to sue. If your registration is made within three months after publication or prior to the infringement, if you win, you can collect both statutory damages and attorney's fees. You can actually register your copyright after an infringement, but if you do, you can only collect actual damages or lost profits—no attorney's fees.

To register a copyright you can order Form TX from the copyright office by mail, or go to their Web site and copy off that form.

> Copyright Office
> Library of Congress
> 101 Independence Ave. SE
> Washington DC 20559–6000
> (202) 707-3000
> http://lcweb.loc.gov/copyright

You will also find additional details about copyright on their Web site. The cost for each registration is thirty dollars.

COPYRIGHT PROTECTION FOR BOOKS

I'm often asked if you sell first rights to a book like you do with an article. Actually, what you sell is book rights, plus any other subsidiary right outlined in the book contract. You don't have to specify the rights offered when you submit a book as you do with a periodical piece. The contract will indicate whether the book is copyrighted in your name (preferred) or in the name of the publisher, which will be negotiable.

KNOW WHAT RIGHTS YOU ARE SELLING

Sally Stuart

FIRST RIGHTS

The right to use a piece of writing for the first time. After it's printed the rights automatically revert to you, and you may offer reprint rights to other publications that accept reprints (see Reprint Rights below).

FIRST SERIAL RIGHTS

"Serial" refers to using a piece in a periodical, so First Serial Rights is first use in a periodical.

FIRST NORTH AMERICAN SERIAL RIGHTS

First use in a periodical in North America.

ONE-TIME RIGHTS

Right to publish one time—not necessarily the first time. This typically refers to sales made to newspapers that have their own designated publication/distribution area, but in Christian publishing it also refers to denominational publications that distribute to their own denominational readership—which does not overlap with other denominations. In other words, you can sell one-time rights to the different denominations simultaneously.

ALL RIGHTS

The publisher buys complete rights and the author forfeits all rights to any further use. The publisher owns the piece and may reprint it or sell to others at will without any further payment to the author. Selling all rights is usually only advisable if the payment is high enough, you want to add the publication to your list of published credits, or there is no other market for the piece. If you sell all rights, they revert to you after thirty-five years. All rights—sometimes called "Exclusive Rights"—cannot be sold unless the transfer is stated specifically in writing. The publisher must indicate in writing that they are buying all rights.

WORK FOR HIRE

Some types of writing that are closely controlled by the publisher, such as curriculum writing, are often sold on a work-for-hire basis. That means the publisher is hiring you to write the material, and the final manuscript belongs to the publisher. Material sold on a work-for-hire basis does not revert to the author after thirty-five years.

REPRINT RIGHTS

If you have previously sold first or one-time rights to a piece of writing and it has been published the first time, the rights then automatically revert to you, and you are free to offer reprint rights to any publications that indicate they are open to reprints. Reprint rights are sometimes referred to as "Second Rights."

SIMULTANEOUS RIGHTS

Selling the right to publish a piece simultaneously to more than one publisher. Generally you reserve this right for sales to non-overlapping markets—such as the denominational markets described above (see One Time Rights). When selling Simultaneous Rights, be sure all parties involved know you are doing so. For example, if you have an article for Christian teens on dealing with peer pressure—that would be of interest to teens in all denominations—you might offer the article simultaneously to the teen periodical for each denomination.

NON-EXCLUSIVE RIGHTS

If you don't specify what rights you are selling, and the publisher doesn't indicate what rights they are buying, you have likely sold non-exclusive rights. This gives them the right to publish the material originally and again in the future in the same periodical—but not in other periodicals put out by the same publisher.

22

FINDING THE RIGHT MARKET

Sally Stuart

*This manuscript of yours that has just come back from
another editor is a precious package. Don't consider it rejected.
Consider that you've addressed it "to the editor who can
appreciate my work" and it has simply come back stamped
"not at this address." Just keep looking for the right address.*

—Barbara Kingsolver

Generally speaking, writers fall into one of two categories: They are creative writers who write for the pure pleasure and challenge of it and have no inclination toward ever seeing their writing published. Or, they write for publication and with a motivating desire to see their words in print.

It is for the latter group that this chapter is written. An alternate title for this chapter could be, "You Don't Have to Market Unless You Want to Get Paid."

Writing for publication is a business, and like any business you must give special attention to the product you have to offer (other chapters in this book deal with developing a good product) and to your market—those customers who are going to buy your stories, articles, poems, books and the like. Our goal here is to teach you how to match that polished product to the editor or publisher who needs it.

TAKING THE TIME TO MARKET

If there is one thing I've learned about marketing over the years, it's that it tends to be a problem—or at least a frustration—for nearly everyone. I've given a lot of thought to why that is, and the conclusion I've reached is that it's about the time. The majority of writers see marketing as a sideline—almost an afterthought to the writing itself. If you've had experience with any kind of a sales-oriented business, you know that marketing the product has to be at the center of everything you do. The same is true with writing. Until you reach the point where you give it the time it deserves, you will continue to struggle with the marketing process.

SETTING YOUR DIRECTION

You first must decide what kind of material you are most capable of and most excited about writing. What ignites your passion? Set a target for what you want to write during the next three to five years. Be specific as far as the types of writing—books, feature articles, children's fiction—and about the topics you are most interested in and qualified to write. Today, more than ever, publishers are demanding that authors have appropriate credentials or have paid their dues by establishing a reputation as a writer who can produce a certain type of writing or who is recognized as an "expert" in their chosen field of writing. Your goal should be to develop the kind of credentials or reputation in your field that brings the editors to you with assignments for articles or books. Focus on your specific writing topics and goals.

I run into first-time authors all the time who are attempting to start out by writing a book. I always recommend they go back and begin with articles or other short pieces. There is a lot to learn about writing that is best learned by creating and polishing those shorter pieces. It also allows you to begin developing your reputation and credentials for writing those books in the future.

Give some thought, too, to whom you are going to write for. Many of the topics you might choose to pursue can be written to a variety of audiences, so don't limit yourself to just one. Most publications target a specific age group or demographic. If you try to write for too broad a market—such as adults—you may miss hitting any target. If the publication is geared to adults who are twenty to forty years old, they aren't going to be interested in an article on retirement—unless it is geared to starting your retirement plans early. Look at your topic and come up with a list of all the potential age groups or audiences that might be interested and hone the material to fit their specific needs.

STUDYING THE MARKET FIRST

The real key to marketing success is finding your markets first and then writing a piece to fit the unique needs of that market (see Chapter 20). Most writers fail because they write an entire article, story, or book first, and then struggle as they try to find a market that fits what they have created. Often there is no good fit for the material in that format.

How much better it is if you find the markets that fit your topics and writing style and write to fit their specific needs. It helps a lot if you know ahead of time what topics they want, the length they prefer, what audience they are targeting, and any special requirements they have—such as lots of anecdotes, personal experiences, or in-depth research. You may not sell every article you write taking this approach, but the odds of success improve greatly. Even the rejected pieces will tell the editor you've done your homework and know exactly what they publish.

TARGETING APPROPRIATE PUBLISHERS

As the author of the *Christian Writers' Market Guide*, I have spent the last twenty-plus years developing a guide that will help writers more easily target the appropriate publishers. In the guide, you will find topical listings that will indicate exactly which publishers are interested in a selection of almost 150 different topics. In the magazine section, the publishers are also broken down by the target audience, so you can select the age group or specific audience and the periodicals listed will match that audience.

Your goal as you use the guide is to start compiling a list of possible publishers for each topic or type of writing you are targeting. For periodicals, you will want to send for their writers' guidelines and a sample copy. For book publishers, send for their writers' guidelines and a copy of their latest catalog. The market guide will tell you the size of envelope and the amount of postage needed for your SASE. If you have Internet access, you can copy the guidelines directly from their Web sites.

CONCERNING SAMPLE COPIES, GUIDELINES, AND CATALOGS

I've known writers over the years who tried to shortcut the marketing process by skipping this step of obtaining and studying the guidelines, copies, and catalogs. They often ask if they really have to pay attention to these things. If you ignore them, you do so at your peril. One of the biggest complaints I get from editors is that many of the writers who submit to them have obviously never seen a copy of their magazine or know what kinds of books they publish.

I recommend that you keep the guidelines in a loose-leaf notebook with alphabetical dividers and keep them close at hand for ready reference. I like to keep the sample periodicals in magazine storage boxes—using a different labeled box for each category being targeted—such as children, teens, pastors, women, etc.

ANALYZING THOSE MARKETS

When those guidelines and sample copies are in hand, you're ready to start the hard work of marketing research. Read the guidelines carefully, and use a highlighter to highlight any passages that either indicate this is a good market for your writing—or that it's not. Then read the sample copy or copies (the more copies you can review, the better) cover to cover. Make notes on any insights that come from that reading. For example, you may write, "likes first-person articles," "has a folksy-friendly tone," or "uses lots of personal experience anecdotes"—anything that will help you fit in if you decide to write for them.

For those that look like good prospects, go a step further and do a closer analysis of what elements the article includes. In the margin next to each paragraph identify the contents: anecdote, case study, statistics, personal experience, narration, quote from an authority, etc. What you are looking for is an indication of how much outside input is expected for a piece for this publication. Generally speaking, the higher the payment, the more research you must do and the more evidence you have to bring in to indicate this is more than just your idea.

As you go through your stack of guidelines and copies, you will be eliminating those that don't fit and adding those you like to your growing list of publications that match your selected topics or types of writing.

MARKETING A BOOK

To find a list of appropriate book publishers, you will go through much the same process. Start with the topical listing for the topic you have selected for your book for a basic list of publishers interested in that topic. Check out their listing in the market guide for additional information and get those catalogs and writers' guidelines. Review the guidelines with that highlighter in hand—highlighting the comments that come across either positively or negatively. Start a list of publishers you want to submit to.

In marketing a book, your goal is to find a publisher known for doing the category of books that you would fit in, but that doesn't already have a book on the specific aspect of the topic that your book will address. For example, my first book was a handbook for Sunday school teachers that covered all the various aspects of teaching a Sunday school class. So when I went looking for a publisher, I needed a publisher known for publishing a wide variety of Christian education resources but that had not published a comprehensive handbook like mine.

What you want is a publisher in the right field—but that has a hole you can fill. Typically a publisher is not going to publish a book that is in direct competition to a book already in their line—so avoid those publishers where your book would compete, rather than compliment.

The way you start to identify the proper publishers is to spend some time perusing those book catalogs you sent for. First, get a feel for the overall contents of the catalog—what kind of books do they publish overall? Are you comfortable with the topics they cover and the theological stance they promote? Next, check to see if they have a good number of books in your topic area, and if so, is there a hole for you to fill? If not, then move on to the next catalog. If so, add them to your list.

With the list in hand, visit your local bookstore to see what you can find on the shelves for your topic and from your selected publishers. Which publisher is best represented? Which have the most appealing titles and covers? Speak to the store's book buyer and ask which publisher he or she thinks of first when ordering books on your topic. Ask which books are currently most popular in your subject area. Those are books you should read and report on in your book proposal.

SUBMITTING FOR PUBLICATION

Once you have lined up a list of potential markets for each category or genre you are going to write in, then you are ready to start submitting. Every time you have an idea for a new project, determine what the best market might be (from your list), review their guidelines and sample copy or catalog. Then go to work on that query, article, or book proposal. You may have a skeleton query or proposal in your computer, but you'll always want to personalize it to reflect the needs or wants of each individual publisher before you submit it.

YOUR BEST
MARKETING RESOURCES

Christian Writers' Market Guide by Sally E. Stuart (Shaw Books). Updated annually and available by the first of each year. Only market guide specifically for the Christian market, with 350 book publishers, nearly 700 periodical publishers, topical listings, agents, groups, conferences, editorial services, contests, and resources. $29.99, plus postage. Go to www.stuartmarket.com

Sally Stuart's Guide to Getting Published by Sally E. Stuart (Shaw Books, 2000). Detailed marketing information, and instructions for writing query letters and book proposals. Special price $14, plus postage. Go to www.stuartmarket.com.

Top 50 Christian Periodical Publishers Packet compiled by Sally E. Stuart. Includes a list of the 50 most writer-friendly publications, with a copy of the guidelines and an analysis sheet for each of those. A great supplement to the *Christian Writers' Market Guide*. Go to www.stuartmarket.com.

Write on Target by Dennis E. Hensley and Holly G. Miller (The Writer Books, 1995). This five-phase program will help you write professionally, sell your material, and map out a plan for lifelong success as a writer. It includes twenty-four exercises and lessons for writers and a glossary of terms commonly used in the publishing world.

www.WritersDigest.com provides a wealth of online resources for writing and marketing including lists of periodicals most open to freelance submissions, plus their "101 Best Web Sites for Writers."

Writers' Market (Writer's Digest Books) Updated annually and available in the fall of the previous year. For those writing in the general market. $29.99. Go to www.writersmarket.com.

23

HOW TO TALK
TO AN EDITOR

Lawrence W. Wilson

*It is largely within your power to determine whether
a publisher will buy your work and whether the
public will buy it once it is released.*

—Judith Applebaum and Nancy Evans, *How to Get Happily Published*

S he looked a little nervous.

As she sat down, she cast a glance over her shoulder, as if someone might be watching. She arranged her papers on the table. She folded her hands. She unfolded her hands. She cleared her throat. After a second or two, she looked up cautiously.

"Thanks for meeting with me," she stammered. "I really appreciate you taking the time; I know you're busy."

She hesitated, as if unsure what to say.

"Um . . . I don't know if I should even be here . . . This is my first writer's conference. I've never actually talked to an editor before."

"Hmm," I wondered. "Should I tell her the truth?"

The truth was that I, too, was a little nervous. As a brand new editor, I also was attending my first writers' conference. Like the aspiring writer across the table, I felt a bit like an imposter. Would anyone find out that I was just an ordinary guy who loved books, enjoyed writing and had finally gotten a break in the publishing business?

"Relax," I said, trying to sound composed. "I'm new at this myself."

Editors are the gatekeepers in the publishing industry. To find its way into print, a manuscript must first pass before their wary eyes. And editors are often busy—managing multiple projects and juggling numerous deadlines. No wonder they seem unapproachable, especially to a novice writer. The myth is that editors are irascible curmudgeons who work hard to keep writers at arm's length.

The reality, however, is quite different. Most editors—like most writers—love both books and talking about book ideas. They are personable and engaging people who resort to the dreaded, impersonal rejection slip only because they are pressed for time.

Here's another little-known secret: Editors are constantly looking for writers. An editor's job depends upon finding fresh voices with publishable ideas. That means editors are always searching for new talent. They're looking for *you!*

Whether face-to-face at a writer's conference or via letter or e-mail, getting your work noticed by an editor is the first step toward getting published. And that first meeting can be an agreeable experience. Here are some things to remember when talking to an editor.

RELAX

Editors have this in common with every writer they interview—they know what it's like to feel insecure and face the possibility of rejection. And like you, they love good writing, believe in the power of the written word, and feel privileged to work in Christian publishing. You have a lot in common.

And remember that editors need writers. So approach an editor with the same confidence you would have in dealing with a business partner or professional colleague. You're both in the same business.

DO SOME HOMEWORK

As an acquisitions editor for a Christian publishing house, I have received manuscripts for projects ranging from physics textbooks to witchcraft instruction manuals. Reviewing them was a waste of my time—and the writers'. Before making an appointment with an editor or submitting your work, learn something about the publishing house the editor represents. Read the writer guidelines and list of editorial needs. Take a look at the Web site and catalog. When you know what the editor is looking for, you'll know which of your ideas is likely to be the best fit.

CREATE A HOOK

Whether you meet with an editor in person or submit your material in writing, your face time will be brief, so it's important to make the most of it. Create a *hook* for your book—a brief statement that clearly conveys the message of your book, its audience, and its intended impact. Often called an *elevator pitch,* this is a statement you should be prepared to rattle off at a moment's notice. It will instantly communicate the essence of your idea to an editor.

BE PROFESSIONAL

Editors must make a living in the writing business and approach their work in a businesslike manner. Writers (I speak as one) are driven by passion, eager for opportunities, and can be impatient with the publishing process. I heard of one editor who took a break between appointments at a writer conference. An eager author followed him into the bathroom, finally shoving a book proposal under the bathroom stall. The editor's response was just what every author longs to hear— in a different setting: "Thank you. This meets a current editorial need."

Editors appreciate writers who approach the business side of writing as simply that—a business. Present yourself and your written materials in a professional manner. Think of your conversation with an editor as a business meeting rather than a beauty contest. Present yourself in a competent way, and your idea will receive ready attention.

BE PREPARED FOR REJECTION

I'll never forget the trepidation with which I submitted my first article. Would the editor like it? Would it be accepted? Or would my value as a writer—my very existence as a human being—be called into question? I was not emotionally prepared for the possibility of rejection.

When you approach an editor, remember that he or she will be evaluating the suitability of your work for a given market, not your validity as a writer or a person. Given the fact that about 1 percent of unsolicited manuscripts find their way into print, nearly all writers must deal with rejection. Be patient, and keep writing.

BE READY TO FOLLOW UP

Deadpan comic Steven Wright quipped, "I'm writing a book . . . I've got the page numbers done." Writers spend a great deal of energy crafting the idea for a book or article and are sometimes taken by surprise when its time to take the next step. If an editor asks to see your proposal, be prepared to send it promptly. If you don't, the editor will wonder if you have time to complete the project.

When you send material following a face-to-face meeting, always write "Requested Material" somewhere on your e-mail or envelope. Since editors meet many writers, it is wise to remind the editor of where and when you met. It is acceptable to include a photo of yourself on your letterhead or business card.

MAKE A FRIEND, NOT A SALE

The publishing enterprise thrives on relationships, and most editors are looking for writers, not just manuscripts. Even if your first meeting with an editor doesn't result in a contract, you can begin building a relationship that may be fruitful for years to come. A meeting with an editor is an opportunity to make a professional contact, not just a sale. Present yourself with poise and confidence, and you will make a favorable impression on the editor. That could lead to a future opportunity with that publisher.

Writing is like golf—lots of people do it on the weekends, but only the pros get paid. When you present yourself in a professional manner to an acquisitions editor, you and your work will be taken seriously. That editor will view you not as a novice writer but as a valued member of the publishing team.

DO'S AND DON'TS FOR SUBMITTING MATERIAL TO AN EDITOR

Lawrence W. Wilson

Submitting written material to an editor need not be intimidating. Follow these simple guidelines and you'll get your message through.

DO—

SUBMIT YOUR BEST WORK

Always put your best foot forward, and never apologize for the quality of your work. "I didn't have much time to work on this" is not what an editor wants to hear.

FOLLOW SUBMISSION GUIDELINES

If the editor prefers e-mail, then send e-mail. If the editor will not accept queries, then don't send one. When you present your materials in a professional manner and follow guidelines closely, your work will stand out.

BE PATIENT WHEN WAITING FOR A REPLY

Editors must manage several projects at one time, and evaluating unsolicited material is not their highest priority. Submit a solid proposal, then be patient as it moves through the publisher's system.

DON'T—

EXPECT A FREE CRITIQUE

While some editors offer a primary reason for rejecting a manuscript ("It's too long," "The focus is wrong for our audience"), none of them have time to critique the hundreds of unsolicited submissions they receive.

ARGUE WITH AN EDITOR WHO DOESN'T UNDERSTAND YOUR IDEA

Good writing stands on its own. If your concept isn't clear on paper, a phone call won't help. When an editor "just doesn't get it," review your work to be sure it communicates clearly.

BECOME DISCOURAGED

Selecting material for publication involves sifting and sorting ideas to find the best fit. If one publisher doesn't accept your work, another might. Keep trying. Reevaluate your idea, refine your writing, and keep submitting.

24

WORKING WITH AN AGENT

Janet Kobobel Grant

When a book leaves your hands, it belongs to God. He may use it to save a few souls or to try a few others, but I think that for the writer to worry is to take over God's business.

—Flannery O'Connor

Writers write books. Publishers publish them. But publishers have a big sea of writers to draw from, and someone needs to serve as your swim instructor, telling you who are the sharks and who are the dolphins, and helping you determine with whom you want to swim. That someone is your agent.

So what's the deal with agents? We'll find out the answer to that question and a number of others you might very well be asking, including: What does an agent do? What do you want to avoid in an agent? And what do you do if you can't find an agent to represent you?

WHAT DOES A GOOD AGENT DO?

A good agent does the following:

- Submits your work to the editors and publishers who are most likely to be interested in what you have to offer.

- Weeds out editors and publishers who are difficult to work with, have little ability to get your book into the marketplace, or are experiencing financial problems.
- Checks with editors after a reasonable time to find out their response to your work.
- Negotiates the terms of your contract.
- Keeps you informed of important developments in the publishing industry.
- Looks over your royalty statements and makes sure payments are being made on time.
- Oversees your book for its entire life, from initial idea to being placed out of print in a way that's most beneficial to you.
- Promotes you and your work to editors and publishers. This can result in unexpected opportunities, such as a publisher approaching you with a book idea.
- Offers professional advice on building a career rather than writing one book at a time.

An agent is a generalist; a writer is a specialist. And that's why writers seldom make good agents for themselves. It's like trying to be an oboe player and a conductor at the same time.

WHAT MAKES A "BAD" AGENT?

You might have noticed that I've described what a "good" agent will do for you. That implies bad agents exist.

Some agents are overworked; others are under qualified. In either case, they can hurt your career. They might not know whom to approach with your project and simply send it to everyone—or to all the wrong places. They might not understand how to negotiate your contract, yet you still will have to live by the obligations in that contract. They might not submit your work at all because they don't have time or because they are concentrating their efforts on more established clients. And they might deal with editors and publishers in ways that would embarrass or abhor you.

HOW DO YOU FIND A GOOD AGENT?

So then the question becomes, how can you tell if someone is a bad agent?

I'd suggest as you choose an agent, that you follow the same routine you would use to find a good plumber or a good doctor. You would be loath just to open the telephone directory, close your eyes, and call the person whose name your finger landed on. You'd ask your friends for a referral.

Whom could you ask about agents? Other writers are a good place to start. Most writers know others who write or belong to a critique group or an e-mail writers' loop. What's the scuttlebutt? Who would the authors you know recommend?

HOW DO YOU KNOW IF AN AGENT IS THE RIGHT ONE FOR YOU?

When an agent expresses interest in representing you, resist the urge to say a quick yes. Find out if this person is a good match for *you*. Like when selecting a doctor, just because a physician has a good reputation doesn't mean you'll have a relationship that works for both of you.

Here's a list of questions to ask:

WHY DID YOU BECOME AN AGENT?

As you listen to the answer, you'll learn about motivations, qualifications, and how he or she relates to writers, editors, and publishers.

WHAT DID YOU DO BEFORE BECOMING AN AGENT?

Try to get a sense of whether the person was successful at past roles, if his or her past connects with being an agent, and why that person left the previous position.

HOW INVOLVED ARE YOU IN WORKING WITH YOUR CLIENTS IN DEVELOPING IDEAS?

Some agents will shop anything you give them; some will work hard to help you formulate your ideas; others like to help you put together your proposals; and some will read your finished manuscript before you send it to your publisher. The level of involvement varies considerably.

Some have editorial backgrounds, some marketing. Each type of expertise will mean a certain type of relationship with clients. An agent who has a marketing background might be happy to talk about the best title for your project but wouldn't want to dip into how the plotline for your novel is developing. But an agent with an editorial background will have a much better sense of whether your synopsis for your mystery has some serious holes.

WHICH HOUSES THAT PUBLISH MY TYPE OF MANUSCRIPT HAVE YOU PLACED PROJECTS WITH?

If you're a children's author, and the agent you're talking to has limited connections in your field, regardless of how much you like the person, it's probably not a good match.

COULD I CONTACT A COUPLE OF YOUR CLIENTS WHO WRITE THE SAME SORT OF WORK I DO?

Most agents will be glad to give you an opportunity to interact with one or two of the authors they represent. You can find out what those clients like about that particular agent and in what ways the agent has helped them with their career.

When all is said and done, having a bad agent is worse than having no agent. After all, who needs to hire someone to create animosity with editors and publishers? Or someone who never gets around to sending out your work? Or someone who can't figure out whom to send it to? Or someone who simply has a very different style of operating from what you're comfortable with? These types of agents don't help your career but hinder it.

HOW DO YOU GET AN AGENT INTERESTED IN YOU?

How do you get an agent to represent you? Here's what I weigh when I make that decision, but the criteria will vary from agent to agent; however, this will give you an idea of how to present yourself.

I ask the following questions:

- Has the person published before? How many books? With which publishers? What were the sales figures?
- Did the person come to me through a recommendation? Who made the recommendation?

- What kind of publishing future might this person have? Is his or her writing strong? Does it stand out from the crowd? Are the ideas creative and marketable? Would the writing have broad appeal, or would it have strong appeal to a select but significant audience?
- Would a number of publishers be interested in the proposal I'm reading, or would just one publisher be interested?
- Is this someone I'd like to work with?
- Do I feel excitement when I read this proposal?

In publishing, you'll find that editors, agents, and yes, even publishers listen to what their instincts tell them about a project. Those who have good instincts are described as having "The Golden Gut"—their "stomach" tells them this is something new, exciting, and very sales-worthy.

For me, I don't have to answer positively all of the above questions to decide to represent someone. Sometimes a yes to just two of those questions can cause me to decide to represent someone. I use my intuition.

Your goal, as a writer, is to give an agent every reason to say yes to you and no reason to say no. Every agent receives hundreds if not thousands of requests to represent authors every month, so the majority of writers who approach agents will be turned down—but for many, they'll find an agent after their careers are established a bit. So don't despair if you need to swim in the publishing ocean for a while by yourself.

As you probably already know, moving from being a writer to being a successful author is a challenging, exciting, arduous, fulfilling, frustrating, and ever surprising venture. Should you be fortunate enough to find a good agent to travel with you down this path, you'll be enriched by the experience. But until that time, I wish you the best in your publishing venture. Now, get out there and knock on some publishing doors!

HOW DO I ACT
AS MY OWN AGENT?

——————— Janet Kobobel Grant ———————

Because few unpublished or recently published authors can find an agent, you can serve as your own agent while you launch your career. Here are a few pointers:

HOW DO I KNOW WHICH HOUSE WOULD
WANT MY MANUSCRIPT?

You can ascertain what type of manuscripts houses publish by perusing market guides such as *Writer's Market, Novel & Short Story Writer's Market, Children's Writer's & Illustrator's Market, Christian Writers' Market Guide.* Many directories of this sort exist to help start you off in the right direction.

Have in mind, as you explore places to submit, what category your manuscript fits in. Make sure your manuscript doesn't straddle categories. Publishers don't know what to do with a science fiction novel that highlights the romance between the hero and heroine. Is it science fiction or is it romance?

Believe a publisher's entry in a directory when it says, "Study our catalog. Know what we publish. Write for guidelines." The number of inappropriate submissions to publishing houses is immense and adds up to a loss of time and energy for both the publishing house and for the author.

Check out a publisher's web site to see what sorts of books it consistently produces. It makes all kinds of sense to submit a book of prayers from various religions that a parent could pray for a child to Harper San Francisco, which has an ecumenical slant to its books. But that project would never interest Tyndale House, which is an evangelical publishing house that would want only Christian prayers.

HOW DO I SEND MY MANUSCRIPT TO A HOUSE?

Once again, directories can guide you as to what a publishing house will accept, and publishers' web sites often have this information, as well. Some publishers want you to send a query letter, in which you inquire about whether they would like to see your manuscript. Some, especially children's book publishers, will look at your entire manuscript. Most will ask for a query letter first, and if the manuscript sounds suitable, the publisher will ask to see a segment of the manuscript. Never send more than is asked for. It's not helpful to mail six children's book when the editor asked for one, or the first one hundred pages when the editor asked for fifty.

HOW DO I FOLLOW UP?

Sometimes directories will indicate the normal amount of time it takes for a publisher to respond to submissions. If so, respect those guidelines. If not, give the publisher at least two months before you ask if the submission arrived and is under review. You may ask via e-mail, if you have an editor's e-mail address, or a phone call. E-mail is preferable because the editor can respond as he or she has time, and sometimes the editor needs to check just where that submission is—after all, hundreds may have arrived the same week as yours.

Always be polite but don't try to engage the person in a continuing dialogue. And remember, being impatient or surly has yet to wring a contract out of an editor.

25

DEVELOPING YOUR PLATFORM

Liz Curtis Higgs

Be sincere; be brief; be seated.

—James Roosevelt

Writing and public speaking have two things in common: both communicate potentially life-changing messages and both use words. But the skills employed by writers and speakers are decidedly different.

Writing is done in private, often alone and in silence, each word weighed and measured as the writer spends countless hours honing the manuscript to perfection.

Speaking is a noisy, public affair, performed in a limited time frame, using much more than words to convey a message. Facial expressions, body language, props and backdrops, dramatic elements, and audience participation all come into play.

For a writer who prefers the company of a computer screen, the thought of developing a speaking platform can be daunting: "Who? *Me* speak?" Yet most publishers are looking for authors who can get the word out about their books. Few ways are more effective than sharing your heartfelt message with a receptive audience.

If you are willing to step out on faith—and onto a platform—here's how to take that giant leap from the page to the stage.

SUBJECT MATTER

Alexander Gregg advises, "Get into your subject, get your subject into you, get your subject into your audience." Your presentation should solve problems, meet needs, offer hope, or in some way make your listeners glad they came. The more interesting your topic is to you, the more interesting it will be for your listeners. Do more research than you will ever need, so your well is full, and you'll have plenty to draw from.

Determine how many points it will take to deliver your message, then create a block of material for each one. I allow about fifteen minutes for each point, such that I can create an hour-long presentation with four main ideas, a forty-five minute version with three, and a half-hour presentation with two. Same topic, same title, just different lengths to meet the programming needs of various groups.

Quotes by famous people are a great way to set apart each section of your speech, including verses of Scripture (by Someone truly famous), which allow you to carry God's Word into the most amazing places. After sharing an appropriate quote, expand upon that thought-provoking statement with interesting, relevant information and suggested application.

STORY TIME

Choose a story to illustrate each point. People don't remember facts and figures; they remember stories and examples—the more personal and original, the better.

A funny incident invites the audience to laugh with you. An embarrassing situation adds an element of risk, since they might laugh *at* you more than with you. Sharing a poignant moment requires even more vulnerability, and offers even more value. Disclosing a painful experience is riskier still, yet often has the greatest impact on the audience, especially if you include the lessons you've learned along the way.

Don't hesitate to include humor and pathos in the same story. Laughter and tears are neighbors, emotionally speaking, and movement back and forth between them is natural. The most serious presentation still needs some comic relief. The most hilarious presentation benefits from a thoughtful moment.

NOTE WORTHY

Using notes lets an audience know you've prepared for their event, instead of delivering a canned speech. I recommend a three-ring notebook, instead of loose sheets of paper, which can get out of order, or note cards, which are easily dropped. Your notes should include only your main points, not a word-for-word manuscript, or you'll be tempted to read it aloud instead of looking at the audience.

Underline key words or phrases with a colorful marker, so those main points will catch your eye as you glance down at the page. Number the pages so you can pace yourself, and divide the material in such a way that you can discreetly turn the page at a point where your listeners might be laughing or jotting down notes, rather than at an emotionally charged moment. Bracket sections that can be skipped if you find yourself running out of time. And memorize your introduction and conclusion for maximum impact.

BATTLING BUTTERFLIES

My first speaking engagement was in front of several hundred folks at my own church. When the dreaded hour arrived, my mouth felt like cotton, my hands had turned to ice, and I mounted that platform with wobbly knees.

If this sounds familiar, take heart: several hundred presentations later, I still battled those same pre-speech jitters. Butterflies are to be expected—let's get them flying in formation.

Send ahead a brief, printed introduction, and bring a copy with you. As you are waiting to be introduced, take a long, deep breath, then let it out slowly. If you're off-stage, touch your toes, stretch out your arms, roll your shoulders. If your mouth is dry as toast, take a sip of room temperature water (ice water constricts the throat), or run the tip of your tongue along the roof of your mouth. (Sounds strange, I know, but it works!)

Above all, pray. Pray not that you will be impressive, but that the audience will be receptive. Pray that your words will make a difference in their lives, and that God's love for them will shine through you. Speaking is all about honoring the Lord and ministering to the audience. It is not about you. That realization alone may help you relax as you stand to speak.

When you reach the podium, resist the urge to start talking immediately. Instead, look right at the audience. Greet them with your eyes. Wait until you—and they—are ready before you begin.

Think conversation, not presentation. Rather than scanning faces or focusing on foreheads, make genuine eye contact with one person at a time and remain there for a full beat. You'll know when a connection is made just by the attentive look on that person's countenance. A slight nod of acknowledgment will assure them, "Yes, I'm talking to *you!*" Then move to another friendly face. Don't let a bored expression or a distracted participant throw you. Find those attendees who are eager to engage with you and let them serve as your true audience. Not only will that exchange build your confidence, but soon everyone else in the room will sense what's happening and feel drawn into your conversation, hoping you'll look at them next . . . and you will!

SPEAKING THE TRUTH IN LOVE

What your audience wants is you . . . the *real* you. Tell the truth, even if it hurts, sounds foolish, or makes people slightly uncomfortable. Love the audience unconditionally without requiring that they love you back. Take risks, try new things, flow with the moment, and let go of the outcome. Manipulation is taking your audience somewhere you aren't willing to go. Vulnerability means going there first, without looking back.

James Roosevelt said, "My father gave me these hints on speech-making: Be sincere, be brief, be seated!" When your time is up, finish. Here's where that memorized ending comes in handy. Audiences remember their first impression of you, but even more, they remember the lasting impression you leave with them, which is often formed in your heartfelt closing words.

GETTING THE WORD OUT

The only way to get into the world of public speaking is to speak— everywhere and anywhere. The audience you stand before is your best source of future engagements—always.

If you want to speak to general audiences, contact local civic clubs like Business and Professional Women, the Junior League, Professional Secretaries International, American Business Women's Association, etc., and offer to do a thirty-minute program in your area of expertise. These groups meet regularly and are always looking for good local speakers, so jump right in. You may be able to find them in the phone book or by tracking down members among your circle of friends. You'll also want to check the business calendar section of your local newspaper for contact information.

If you feel called to speak to Christian audiences, churches also have various groups that meet on a regular basis—men, women, teens, senior adults, young mothers, single adults, etc.—eager to find speakers who bring an inspirational message centered on the Lord and his Word.

For either kind of organization, provide a one-sheet biography, a one-sheet topic description, and a digital photo to use in publicizing your presentation. As soon as you've prepared a solid thirty- to sixty-minute program, start making phone calls. If you are uncomfortable offering your services over the telephone, simply call to determine the name and address of the contact person, then send him or her the above information with a personal note of introduction.

HONORABLE HONORARIUMS

Many beginning speakers worry about what they should charge for their services. That's a very individual decision based on your talents, your experience, and the demand for your services. Few people who want to create a long-term career in public speaking can avoid doing lots of freebies in the beginning. When it's time to establish an honorarium, choose an amount that is fair to all involved, and quote the same fee to everyone—speakers call it "fee integrity." As experience and demand dictate, your speaking fee can inch upward, although your greatest goal should be to provide the right message for the right audience and honor the Lord from first word to last.

FROM PAGE TO STAGE

Liz Curtis Higgs

Few things can undo a well-prepared presentation like an ill-designed speaking environment. As soon as you arrive, check the room for these potential problems, and don't hesitate to ask your meeting planner for help solving them. They want what *you* want: a successful presentation.

DIM LIGHTING

If the audience cannot see you, they'll have trouble following your message. And if you cannot see them, you'll have a hard time maintaining eye contact. Ask for the house lights to be turned up and for the staging area to be well lit. A simple flick of a light switch can make all the difference.

DEATH VALLEY

"Death Valley" is a clever name for that broad, empty expanse between the podium and the first row of chairs, where many speeches die an early death. Bridge the gap by moving the lectern forward or pulling the chairs closer to the front. Rather than sitting in your seat, feeling nervous beforehand, welcome people as they enter the room and encourage them to fill those front chairs. Make a special effort to greet those seated in your first row. Their enthusiasm and energy will help fuel your delivery.

BANGING DOORS

These are especially distracting in a small meeting room. Request that all the doors be closed a few moments before the program is to begin, leaving the farthest one propped open for those inevitable latecomers, who can slip in unobtrusively.

ANNOYING CELL PHONES

Ask your introducer to request that all cell phones be turned off or adjusted to ring silently. Often a brief demonstration (having someone intentionally call the introducer's cell phone during the opening remarks) makes the point in a light-hearted but effective way.

MISBEHAVING MICROPHONES

The microphone is your friend: hold it close to your mouth and speak directly into it. A hand-held microphone, rather than a clip-on style, allows you to move around with ease, and to reach for a replacement microphone if there are technical difficulties, instead of fumbling around with switches clipped behind your back.

What to do when you hear the telltale squeal of feedback? Try moving away from the speakers—often found in the ceiling above you—or stepping slightly away from the lectern, which may be reflecting sound back into the microphone. Having the person in charge turn down the volume is another option.

Whatever you do, don't ignore the problem of feedback; that ringing sound will leave your audience cringing instead of listening. If it's working properly, *use* the microphone, rather than assuming you can be heard without it. The audience that can hear and see you is a happy audience.

Control what you can, but don't let less-than-ideal circumstances throw you. Sometimes you can't change the room, but you can always change you. When it comes to public speaking, ego is the biggest obstacle of all.

CONTRIBUTORS

Karen Ball is an award winning author, editor, and speaker, and has worked in publishing for more than twenty years. Currently executive editor of fiction at Zondervan Publishing House, she has had the honor of working with such authors as Francine Rivers, Robin Jones Gunn, Liz Curtis Higgs, Terri Blackstock, Gilbert Morris, Angela Elwell Hunt, and Bill Myers. Karen's newest full-length novel, *Shattered Justice*, was released in June 2005.

James Scott Bell is the best-selling author of *Deadlock, Breach of Promise,* and *Glimpses of Paradise,* as well as *Write Great Fiction: Plot & Structure.* A winner of the Christy Award for Excellence in Christian Fiction, Jim is a columnist for *Writer's Digest* magazine and teaches fiction at Pepperdine University.   *www.jamesscottbell.com*

Jerry Brecheisen (pronounced "Breck-eye-zen") is the author of fourteen books, including *The Winning Dad* and *When Life Doesn't Turn Out the Way You Expect,* and he has edited or compiled thirty other books, manuscripts, and audiovisual scripts. His weekly column, *Hope Above the Headlines,* offers a humorous and positive application of biblical principles to current headlines.   *www.brecksong.com*

Keith Drury is the author of more than a dozen books and manuals published and translated into English, Spanish, French, and Japanese. Some of his more widely circulated books are *Holiness for Ordinary People, Spiritual Disciplines for Ordinary People,* and *With Unveiled Faces.* He teaches at Indiana Wesleyan University
                                          www.drurywriting.com/keith

Sharon Norris Elliott is a Christian educator, conference speaker, composer, author, assistant director of the Sandy Cove Writers' Conference, and Advisory Board Member of American Christian Writers. She is the author of *What? Teenagers in the Bible* and *The Stupid Term Paper: How to Plan It, Write It, and Get an A on It.*

www.sharonnorriselliott.com

James L. Garlow is an author, communicator, and historian who serves as senior pastor of Skyline Wesleyan Church in San Diego, California. His daily radio commentary, *The Garlow Perspective*, is heard daily on over three hundred radio stations. He is the best-selling author of *Cracking DaVinci's Code* and *God Still Heals.*

www.jimgarlow.com

Janet Kobobel Grant is an author and literary agent representing best-selling authors such as Robin Jones Gunn and Rene Gutteridge. Janet's own books include *The Breast Cancer Care Book, Experiencing God's Presence, Facing Life's Uncertainties, Growing in Prayer,* and *Trusting God Will Provide.*   *www.booksandsuch.biz*

Dennis E. Hensley holds four degrees in communications, including a Ph.D. in English from Ball State University. He is a full professor of English at Taylor University Fort Wayne, where he serves as director of the professional writing major. He is the author of forty-five books, including eight textbooks on writing and six novels. He is a board member of Christian Writers Guild, a judge for the annual Christy Fiction Awards and for the Evangelical Press Association awards, and a columnist and contributing editor with *Writers' Journal* and *Advanced Christian Writer.* He has sold more than three thousand freelance newspaper and magazine articles.

Liz Curtis Higgs is an internationally known speaker and the author of twenty-two books with more than three million copies in print, including the best-selling novel *Thorn in My Heart* and the best-selling non-fiction book *Bad Girls of the Bible.* In 1995 Liz received the Council of Peers Award for Excellence from the National Speakers Association, becoming one of only forty women in the world named to the CPAE Speaker Hall of Fame.   *www.lizcurtishiggs.com*

Bob Hostetler is the recipient of two Gold Medallion Book Awards, three Ohio Associated Press Awards, and an Amy Foundation Award and has twenty books to his credit. He has co-authored eleven books with Josh McDowell, including the best-selling *Right from Wrong (What You Need to Know to Help Youth Make Right Choices)* and the award-winning *Don't Check Your Brains at the Door.*   *www.bobhostetler.com*

Hal Hostetler is a retired managing editor of *Guideposts* magazine and is now a roving editor and teacher of writing. This former newspaperman helped smuggle Bibles into Communist countries with Brother Andrew.

Julie-Allyson Ieron (pronounced "I-run") is the author of four books including *Praying Like Jesus* and *Staying True in a World of Lies*. She is a former managing editor of Moody Press, senior editor of *Moody* magazine, and managing editor of *The Standard* magazine. Julie currently manages her own writing and public relations company and serves as an acquisitions editor for Christian Publications Inc. She is a mentor and master craftsman with the Jerry B. Jenkins Christian Writers Guild.

Jerry B. Jenkins is the best-selling author of the *Left Behind* series as well as 150 other books, including, assisting with *Just As I Am: The Autobiography of Billy Graham*. Formerly vice-president of publishing for the Moody Bible Institute, Dr. Jenkins owns the Christian Writers Guild and Jenkins Entertainment, a filmmaking company in Los Angeles that produced the critically acclaimed *Hometown Legend*. Jerry's articles have appeared in *TIME, Reader's Digest, Writer's Digest, Parade, Guideposts,* and dozens of Christian periodicals. *www.jerryjenkins.com*

Ron McClung is a district superintendent in The Wesleyan Church and coauthor of *1–2 Timothy, Titus, Philemon: A Commentary for Bible Students*. He writes the weekly column *Positive Perspective*.

Cecil "Cec" Murphey is the author of more than one hundred books and six hundred articles. He has written, co-written, or ghostwritten books for such well-known personalities as Ben Carson (*Gifted Hands*), Franklin Graham, and Joyce Meyer. His most recent best-seller is *90 Minutes in Heaven*, written for Don Piper. Two of his books have been optioned for film. Cec is a popular conference speaker who has taught throughout North America and overseas. *www.cecmurphey.com*

Bonnie Perry is director of Beacon Hill Press of Kansas City. She holds degrees in journalism and English from the University of Missouri. A popular speaker at writers' conferences, she is also the author of many articles and books, including *A Dangerous Hope: Encountering the God of Grace*.

Andy Scheer is managing editor of Jerry B. Jenkins Christian Writers Guild. Andy began his editing career in 1976 at a daily newspaper, then worked for a professional journal. He served for eighteen years with *Moody* magazine and was managing editor from 1990 to 2002. A journalism graduate of Colorado State University, he also studied at Denver Seminary.

Sally Stuart is the leading authority on Christian writing markets. She is the author of thirty-three books, including the annual *Christian Writers' Market Guide* and *Sally Stuart's Guide to Getting Published*. She has also sold over one thousand articles and columns and writes the marketing columns for *The Christian Communicator* and *The Advanced Christian Writer*. *www.stuartmarket.com*

Stan Toler is senior pastor of Trinity Church of the Nazarene in Oklahoma City, Oklahoma, and hosts the television program *Leadership Today*. He trains pastors and church leaders throughout North America with seminars on strategic planning, stewardship, outreach, and leadership. Stan has authored dozens of books including manuals on church ministry, evangelism, and resources for pastors. *www.stantoler.com*

James N. Watkins is an award-winning author and speaker who has written eleven books and contributed to twelve others, winning a *Campus Life* Book of the Year award, a *Christian Retailing* Retailers Choice Award, and four Evangelical Press Association awards. His more than fifteen hundred articles have appeared in *Campus Life, Christianity Today, Decision, Focus on the Family, Leadership, Today's Christian Woman,* and over fifty other publications. He also writes a weekly column for three newspapers, which received an Amy Award for biblical content in a secular publication. *www.jameswatkins.com*

Denise Williamson is the author of six books, including the critically-acclaimed *The Dark Sun Rises* and *When Stars Begin to Fall*, which echo her passion for racial reconciliation. She has served as assistant director of the Sandy Cove Christian Writers' Conference for over ten years.

Lawrence W. Wilson is editorial director at Wesleyan Publishing House and the author of *Why Me? Straight Talk about Suffering*. He has written, contributed to, or compiled more than twenty other books. His syndicated column, *Front Porch*, appears in newspapers across the United States and Canada. *www.lawrencewilson.com*

Norman G. Wilson is the general editor for The Wesleyan Church and executive editor of *Wesleyan Life* magazine. He has been the speaker on the international radio broadcast *The Wesleyan Hour* since its inception in 1975. He is the author of a dozen books including *The Call to Contentment, Follow the Leader,* and *People Just Like Us.*